The Flying Cook

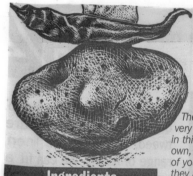

POTATO CAKES WITH FETA AND CHIVES

*Serves six. Prep time: 20 mins.
Cook time: 15-20 mins.*

These savoury little Greek potato cakes go very well with the chicken recipe that will appear in this column tomorrow. As a course on their own, serve with a green leaf salad and some of your favourite relish on the side. I find that they also make perfect hot hor's d'ouvres if they are made a little smaller and rolled in toasted fine breadcrumbs before baking.

Ingredients

Olive oil *for baking*
500 g potatoes, *boiled, mashed*
25g unsalted butter, *melted*
1 egg yolk
3 tblsp chopped fresh parsley
1 tsp fresh oregano, *finely chopped*
4 spring onions, *finely sliced*
100g feta cheese, *crumbled*
3 tsp lemon juice
salt and pepper to taste
6 tblsp lightly toasted fine breadcrumbs.

METHOD

Set the oven to gas mark 5/375f/190c. Lightly oil two baking sheets and pre-heat them in the oven. Pass the mashed potato through a mouli or a fine sieve. Mix the butter with the egg yolk and add to the potato with the parsley, oregano, spring onions, feta cheese and lemon juice. Salt and pepper to taste, remembering that feta cheese is quite salty. Flour your hands and pat the mixture into little cakes about 3cm round. Press each side into the lightly-toasted, fine breadcrumbs and place on the prepared baking sheet. Brush with a little oil and cook for 15-20 minutes, turning over once. Serve warm.

Each day we publish a dish that you can make by itself for a family meal, or as part of our weekly dinner party menu.
Tomorrow: Chicken Cacciatore

DEDICATION

For Jeannie, Steven and Janine for their
inspiration and support
and for Plum.
I would also like to thank 'The Agency'
in the Isle of Man,
Gareth Jones of Granada Television,
Wendy Hobson for editorial support,
Frank Phillips, the book designer, and
Jennifer Jones of BBC Enterprises.

The Flying Cook

KEVIN WOODFORD

NETWORK BOOKS

KEVIN WOODFORD, presenter of the FLYING COOK, is a food consultant to several International Companies. He is presenter and author of *Microwave Maestro* for Granada Television and the *Reluctant Cook* for BBC Television. He is a contributing food writer to several regional newspapers and broadcasts regularly on regional TV and radio.

Front cover and inside photography: James Murphy
Stylist: Jane Mcleish
Home economist: Jacqueline Clark

Published by Network Books,
a division of BBC Enterprises Limited,
Woodlands, 80 Wood Lane, London W12 0TT
First published 1992
© Kevin Woodford 1992
ISBN 0 563 36277 4

Set in Trump Mediaeval
by Ace Filmsetting Ltd, Frome, Somerset
Printed and bound in Great Britain by Clays Ltd, St Ives plc
Colour separations by Technik Ltd, Berkhampstead
Colour printed by Lawrence Allen Ltd, Weston-super-Mare, Avon
Cover printed by Clays Ltd, St Ives plc

CONTENTS

Introduction

'The universal art and science of cookery must create different problems not only to different people but also in different situations.'

It was this statement, made during a luncheon meeting between the Editor and Deputy Editor of *This Morning* and myself which led to *The Flying Cook* being developed.

It was obvious that there was a need for a Culinary Batman, a Gastronomic Superhero, a Sylvester Stallone of the kitchen. Whatever his title, the role was clear – to respond urgently to a potential culinary disaster. This was to be a real 'kitchen sink drama'.

As the 'think tank' delved further into this exciting new project, we hit a gem of an idea. Our hero must respond rapidly to the distress call – 'a helicopter, that's what he needs'.

Now, up to this moment, I was most enthusiastic about the project but it was at this point that I began to chant the names of other television cooks who might be suitable for the role. Not that I'm a wimp, you understand, simply that having only just accepted fixed-wing transportation as being relatively safe yet essentially important – the notion of rotor blades shaving the top of my head while hovering a couple of hundred feet above ground did not appeal to me. But, after some sweet muttering from 'The Management', I was soon persuaded that I was the man for the job. My first encounter with the helicopter was on a damp, miserable sort of day in darkest Cheshire. After several cups of coffee and a lengthy conversation with the pilot, Stafford Pemberton, mainly checking out the condition of his health, number of flying hours and testing his desire to live, we ventured to the machine.

I had been given great awareness of the advanced technology that is involved in helicopters and therefore was unconcerned when after several attempts at starting the engines, it was declared that the damp weather was to blame. After several more attempts, even I, a cook, who does not understand engines, let alone aeronautics – was now afloat.

It took a film crew of five to force me into the cockpit and strap me in, and by then it was too late for me to escape. We were up, up and away. Advanced Technology indeed! But I have to say, after five minutes, I was won over. In the very experienced and safe hands of Stafford, it was obvious that this was to be the most enjoyable cookery programme that I had made to date.

This book explores twelve different situations which many of us experience at some time in our lives, and offers some culinary help to suit our lifestyle. The recipes, which are well tried and tested, have been tailored to the specific topic within which they are presented, although you will find that many are interchangeable. It should be used just as any good cookery book – regularly! One final comment. I make no guarantee for the outcome of serving the recipes in 'Seduction Cuisine', but wish you well!

About the Recipes

Here are a few points to note about the recipes.

- Most recipes are designed to serve 4 people, unless otherwise specified.

- Spoon measurements are level.

- Size 3 eggs are used for the recipes.

- Ovens vary considerably, so adjust cooking times, if necessary, to suit your particular oven.

- Taste as you cook, and adjust seasoning to suit your own personal preference.

- Wash fruits and vegetables before you prepare them.

- Where herbs are listed as chopped or snipped, fresh herbs are best. If you do use dried herbs, use only half the quantity.

COLLEGE CUISINE

Those were the times. Late starts to the day and even later finishes, and somewhere along the way, food of some sort. For many college students, the prospect of having to prepare a meal is not only a daunting prospect, but also an inefficient use of time. The recipes given in this chapter take those considerations into account and are designed to minimise effort whilst maximising the results. They are also written with nutrition in mind. It goes without saying that prolonged bad eating habits could have a detrimental effect upon academic performance.

So, put the tin of baked beans back into the cupboard and have a try at some of these easy-to-produce dishes and just watch how confidently you tackle the next essay!

CHINESE SPARE RIBS

Real sticky-finger cookery, this – make sure you have a bowl of warm water and a clean napkin close to hand when eating this dish.

SERVES 2–4

1 tablespoon vegetable oil
2 tablespoons golden syrup
1 tablespoon dark soy
  sauce
1 small glass sherry
½ teaspoon five-spice
  powder
A pinch of salt
2 tablespoons orange juice
1½ lb (750 g) pork spare
  ribs

1. Mix together all the marinade ingredients.

2. Place the spare ribs in a shallow dish and add the marinade. Leave for at least 2 hours, turning twice.

3. Transfer the ribs on to a grilling tray and grill for 8 to 12 minutes until cooked through.

French Onion Soup

There are not many soups to compete with a good French onion. It's cheap to make both in cost of food and economy of effort, and yet with some good crusty bread can be a meal in itself.

SERVES 4

3 oz (75 g) butter
2 lb (1 kg) onions, peeled
  and sliced
2 cloves garlic, peeled and
  crushed
1 heaped tablespoon plain
  flour
2½ pints (1.5 litres) good
  brown beef stock, hot
Salt and freshly ground
  black pepper
1 tablespoon chopped
  parsley
4 slices crusty white bread
3 oz (75 g) Gruyère cheese,
  grated

1. Heat the butter in a heavy-based pan and add the onions and garlic. Cook for about 15 to 20 minutes, stirring frequently, until the onions are light brown in colour.

2. Add the flour and mix well to absorb all the butter. Cook gently for 3 to 4 minutes.

3. Gradually add the hot stock and simmer for 20 minutes, then remove any surplus fat that has risen to the surface of the soup.

4. Season with salt and freshly ground black pepper and add the parsley.

5. Toast the bread and top the pieces with the grated cheese. Place back under the grill to brown.

6. Pour the soup into individual bowls and top with the cheese toasties.

BAKED POTATO SKINS
WITH CHIVE AND GARLIC DRESSING

This is a tasty and economical recipe. If you are really hard up at the end of a financial term you could ask your friends to save their potato peelings for you. That's what friends are for!

SERVES 2–4

2 tablespoons
  Worcestershire sauce
½ teaspoon tabasco sauce
2 tablespoons dark soy
  sauce
1 tablespoon vegetable oil
Salt and freshly ground
  black pepper
1 lb (450 g) potato peelings,
  washed
6 fl oz (175 ml) single
  cream or plain yoghurt
2 cloves garlic, peeled and
  crushed
2 tablespoons snipped
  chives
A pinch of paprika
Juice of ½ lemon

1. Place the Worcestershire, tabasco and soy sauces with the oil in a bowl and mix well. Add salt and freshly ground black pepper. Soak the potato skins in the marinade for 15 minutes.

2. Pre-heat the oven to gas mark 6, 400°F (200°C).

3. Remove the potato skins to a dry roasting tin and cook in the oven for about 30 minutes.

4. Prepare the dressing by mixing together the cream or yoghurt, garlic, chives, paprika and lemon juice. Season to taste with salt and freshly ground black pepper.

5. Serve the potato skins with the yoghurt dip in front of the telly!

SPAGHETTI IN HAM AND TOMATO SAUCE

Pasta should always be cooked 'al dente'. You can test this by 'nipping' the spaghetti between your thumb and forefinger; it should break cleanly and not be too soft.

SERVES 4

12 oz (350 g) spaghetti
2 oz (50 g) butter
3 oz (75 g) onions, peeled and diced
2 cloves garlic, peeled and crushed
1 tablespoon chopped fresh oregano (or 1 teaspoon dried)
½ bay leaf
1 × 14-oz (400-g) tin chopped tomatoes
2 oz (50 g) tomato purée
A dash of Worcestershire sauce
A pinch of sugar
Salt and freshly ground black pepper
3 oz (75 g) cooked ham, diced
3 oz (75 g) Parmesan cheese, grated

1. Cook the spaghetti in plenty of boiling salted water. Drain and refresh under cold water.

2. Heat the butter and add the onions, garlic, oregano and bay leaf. Cook without colouring the onions for 2 minutes.

3. Add the chopped tomatoes, tomato purée and season with the Worcestershire sauce, sugar, salt and freshly ground black pepper.

4. Re-heat the spaghetti either in a microwave or by immersing in boiling water, or quickly sauté in a little hot butter in a shallow frying pan.

5. Place the spaghetti on a serving dish, pour over the sauce and sprinkle the ham over the top.

6. Serve with a little grated Parmesan cheese.

HAM AND RED PEPPER RISOTTO

Risotto should be sticky and not dry like many rice dishes. This is achieved by using arborio rice (usually called risotto rice) and by stirring it during the cooking process. This releases the starch in the rice and makes the grains stick together.

SERVES 4

1 oz (25 g) butter
1 small onion, peeled and
  finely diced
15 fl oz (450 ml) Italian
  arborio rice
4 oz (100 g) cooked ham,
  sliced and diced
2 red peppers, deseeded and
  sliced
2½ pints (1.5 litres) chicken
  stock, hot
Salt and freshly ground
  black pepper
1 oz (25 g) Parmesan
  cheese, grated

1. Melt the butter in a heavy-based pan, add the onion and cook for 2 to 3 minutes. Add the rice and stir for a further 3 minutes.

2. Add the ham and peppers, then gradually add the chicken stock. Season with salt and freshly ground black pepper.

3. Allow the rice to cook very gently over a medium heat, stirring frequently, for about 25 to 30 minutes.

4. Once the rice is creamy and most of the stock has been absorbed, check to ensure that the grains are cooked and check and adjust the seasoning if necessary.

5. Stir in the Parmesan cheese and serve immediately.

Rapid Pizza

This recipe uses wholewheat flour to give a denser pizza base.

SERVES 2 LARGE PORTIONS

8 oz (225 g) wholewheat
  flour
A pinch of salt
½ teaspoon chopped
  tarragon
½ teaspoon chopped
  parsley
1 teaspoon dried yeast
5 fl oz (150 ml) water,
  warm
1 teaspoon caster sugar

For the topping:
2 fl oz (50 ml) olive oil
3 oz (75 g) onions, peeled
  and finely chopped
1 clove garlic, peeled and
  crushed
1 teaspoon chopped parsley
½ teaspoon chopped
  chervil
Freshly ground black
  pepper
1 × 14-oz (400-g) tin
  chopped tomatoes
1 heaped tablespoon
  tomato purée
1 teaspoon Worcestershire
  sauce
2 drops tabasco sauce
A pinch of caster sugar
Parmesan cheese, grated
2 oz (50 g) Italian salami,
  chopped
1 tablespoon chopped
  parsley

1. Mix together the flour, salt, tarragon and parsley. Place the yeast, water and sugar in a bowl, mix well and cover. Leave this to begin fermenting (about 8 to 10 minutes should do).

2. Add the yeast mixture to the flour and mix to a smooth paste. Transfer to a lightly greased 8-in (20-cm) sandwich tin and press it in firmly. Leave the dough to ferment for 20 minutes.

3. Pre-heat oven to gas mark 7, 425°F (220°C).

4. Heat the olive oil in a heavy-based pan, add the onions and garlic and cook until soft. Season with the herbs and freshly ground black pepper. Add the chopped tomatoes, cook gently for 3 minutes and mix in the tomato purée. Season with the Worcestershire sauce, tabasco sauce and sugar. Allow to cook very gently for 15 minutes or until it develops a fairly thick consistency.

5. Gently promote the dough up the sides of the cake tin, leaving a well on the base on which to pour the tomato mixture. Sprinkle on the cheese and salami.

6. Bake in the oven for about 20 minutes and garnish with a little chopped parsley before serving.

YORKSHIRE PUDDING
FILLED WITH CURRIED BEEF

This is a very substantial meal. You can vary the filling as much as you like; for example, why not use the goulash recipe on page 94, the stew on page 14, the casserole on page 102, or the chilli on page 26 as fillings!

SERVES 4

1 tablespoon vegetable oil
6 oz (175 g) topside of beef,
  cut into cubes
2 oz (50 g) onion, peeled
  and sliced
1 clove garlic, peeled and
  crushed
2 oz (50 g) carrot, peeled
  and diced
2 oz (50 g) celery, sliced
2 oz (50 g) leek, sliced
1½ oz (40 g) curry powder
1 oz (25 g) plain flour
  (optional)
1 oz (25 g) tomato purée
2 oz (50 g) mango chutney
1¼ pint (750 ml) beef stock
2 oz (50 g) apple, peeled,
  cored and diced
½ oz (15 g) desiccated
  coconut

For the pudding:
3 oz (75 g) plain flour
1 egg
3 fl oz (75 ml) milk
2 fl oz (50 ml) water
Salt and freshly ground
  black pepper
Vegetable oil or beef
  dripping

1. Heat the oil in a heavy-based pan, add the beef and fry, turning frequently, to seal the meat.

2. Add the onion, garlic, carrot, celery and leek and cook for 2 minutes.

3. Dust the ingredients with curry powder to taste and, if necessary, a little flour if there appears to be an excessive amount of fat in the pan. Mix well.

4. Stir in the tomato purée, mango chutney and stock.

5. Add the apple and coconut, bring to the boil and simmer for 45 to 60 minutes.

6. Pre-heat the oven to gas mark 7, 425°F (220°C).

7. Meanwhile, prepare the Yorkshire pudding by sifting the flour into a large bowl. Add the egg and beat, then slowly beat in the milk, water and seasoning.

8. Place a little oil or dripping in a 7-in (18-cm) round cake tin and place in the oven for 10 minutes.

9. Add the batter to the tin and leave to cook on the highest shelf for about 25 to 30 minutes until golden brown and crisp.

10. Transfer to a large plate and fill with the curry.

RELUCTANT COOK
BROWN BEEF STEW

This is the classic beef stew with vegetables, whether its title is in English or French. As with all slow-cooked dishes, once you've done the initial preparation you bung all the ingredients into the casserole and come back later to a delicious, steaming-hot dish. The flavouring vegetables and the meat can simply braise undisturbed in the hot liquid.

SERVES 4

1½ lb (750 g) topside of
  beef, cut into 1-in (2.5-cm)
  cubes
1 medium onion, peeled
  and roughly chopped
2 carrots, peeled and sliced
  into thin rounds
3 stalks celery, sliced into
  ½-in (1-cm) pieces
1 large leek, halved
  lengthways and thinly
  sliced
3 tablespoons vegetable oil
½ tablespoon plain flour
2–3 tablespoons tomato
  purée
1 clove garlic, peeled and
  crushed
1 pint (600 ml) beef stock,
  hot
4 fl oz (120 ml) red wine
1 bouquet garni
Salt and freshly ground
  black pepper

1. Prepare the meat and vegetables itemised in the main list of ingredients (not the garnish vegetables).

2. Pre-heat the oven to gas mark 6, 400°F (200°C).

3. Heat the oil over a medium heat in a heavy flameproof casserole and, when it is hot, add the meat. Fry the meat for 2 to 3 minutes, stirring constantly, until lightly browned on all sides.

4. Add all the prepared vegetables (except the garlic) from the main ingredients list. Fry for 3 to 4 minutes, stirring, then sprinkle in the flour, mix well and fry for 2 to 3 minutes.

5. Add the tomato purée and garlic and stir thoroughly. Ladle in the stock gradually, mixing after each addition, then pour in the wine. Finally add the bouquet garni and season with salt and freshly ground black pepper.

6. Cover the casserole with a tight-fitting lid and cook in the oven for about 1½ hours.

7. About 30 minutes before the end of the cooking time, bring 2 pans of water to the boil. Meanwhile, prepare the garnish

For the garnish:

8 oz (225 g) button onions, peeled

8 oz (225 g) turnips, peeled and diced

8 oz (225 g) carrots, peeled and diced

8 oz (225 g) potatoes, peeled and diced

1 tablespoon butter

vegetables, making sure that they are all cut into pieces of the same size so that they take the same length of time to cook.

8. About 15 minutes before the end of the cooking time, start to cook the garnish vegetables. Put the onions, turnips and carrots into one of the pans and simmer until the turnips are cooked through but not soft, by which time the other vegetables should be cooked too. Put the potatoes in the other pan and boil until they are cooked but not falling apart.

9. Drain all the cooked garnish vegetables together and put into one pan with the butter. Cover and set aside.

10. Remove the stew from the oven, discard the bouquet garni and check the consistency of the sauce. It should be fairly thick so that it will coat the back of a spoon. If it is too thin, place the casserole, uncovered, over a medium heat and stir constantly so that the extra liquid evaporates. If the sauce is too thick, add extra stock or red wine and cook over medium heat for an extra 5 minutes. Check and adjust the seasoning if necessary.

11. You can either serve the stew straight from the casserole with the garnish vegetables on top, or pour it into a warmed serving dish and place the vegetables around the edges.

SHEPHERD'S PIE

College days conjure up thoughts of piping hot creamy mashed potato lovingly laid upon savoury mince, and a glass of ice-cold lager.

SERVES 4

2 tablespoons oil or
  cooking fat
4 oz (100 g) celery, chopped
3 medium carrots, peeled
  and chopped
1 onion, peeled and
  chopped
1 lb (450 g) minced beef
2 tablespoons tomato purée
2 tablespoons plain flour
8 fl oz (250 ml) beef stock
Salt and freshly ground
  black pepper
1 lb (450 g) potatoes, peeled
  and quartered
1 oz (25 g) butter

1. In a medium saucepan, heat the oil or fat over medium heat. Add the vegetables and cook for 2 to 3 minutes, stirring with a wooden spoon.

2. Add the minced beef and break it up with the spoon. Cook the meat, stirring constantly, until it loses its pink colour.

3. Add the tomato purée and mix it in well. Then add the flour and mix well. Make sure that all the fat has been absorbed by the flour. Cook the mixture, stirring, for a few more minutes to cook the flour thoroughly.

4. Slowly add the stock, a ladleful at a time, stirring after each addition. Once all the stock has been added, season sparingly with salt and freshly ground black pepper.

5. Transfer the mixture to a clean pan. Turn the heat up so that the mixture bubbles gently. Leave it to cook, uncovered, for 20 to 25 minutes. It will thicken as the liquid evaporates. Check from time to time that the mixture isn't sticking to the pan and burning. If it is, add a little water, stir well, and keep stirring occasionally.

6. Put the potatoes in a saucepan and cover them with water. Bring quickly to the boil, turn down the heat and simmer the potatoes for 15 to 20 minutes or until soft.

7. When the potatoes are cooked, drain them and return them to the pan. Mash them by pushing them through a sieve or by using a fork or potato masher, getting rid of all the lumps. Add the butter and mix thoroughly.

8. Pre-heat the oven to gas mark 6, 400°F (200°C).

9. The meat mixture should be very thick by now. Spoon it into a deep ovenproof dish. Cover it with the mashed potatoes. Place the dish in the oven.

10. Heat through until the top is brown. Serve at once.

APPLE AND CINNAMON CRUMBLE

This is one of my favourite puddings. It's lovely when accompanied by fresh cream, custard or home-made ice-cream and either summer fruits or winter berries, depending on the time of the year.

SERVES 4

2 lb (900 g) cooking apples, peeled, cored and sliced
1 oz (25 g) soft brown sugar
½ teaspoon cinnamon
3 fl oz (75 ml) dry cider

For the crumble:
8 oz (225 g) plain flour, sieved
3 oz (75 g) butter
Grated zest of 1 lemon
5 oz (150 g) soft brown sugar

1. Place the apples, sugar, cinnamon and cider in a saucepan and allow to cook gently until the apple slices are soft.

2. Transfer the mixture into an earthenware pie dish.

3. Pre-heat the oven to gas mark 4, 350°F (180°C).

4. Place the flour in a mixing bowl, add the butter and lemon zest and gently rub into the flour. Once it appears light and crumbly then gently mix in the sugar.

5. Top the apples with the crumble mix without compressing it. Bake in the oven for 25 to 30 minutes until golden brown.

SURVIVAL CUISINE

This chapter includes recipes which are relatively adventurous yet simple to follow and require very little effort to produce. Survival cuisine is do to with looking after your gastronomic needs when perhaps your partner has gone away for a short while, leaving you to fend for yourself. The easy solution is, of course, to buy a season ticket to the local Chinese restaurant, or worse still, the 'chippy' just around the corner. Well, by following these recipes, you'll soon have the owner of the local Chinese restaurant knocking on your door, driven there by the aroma of beautiful food, to steal your culinary secrets.

CREAM OF PEA SOUP

It's amazing what you can do with a bag of defrosted peas! Of course – it's far better to use fresh shelled peas but if it's a matter of survival, don't be afraid to open the freezer.

SERVES 4–6

2 oz (50 g) butter
3 oz (75 g) bacon, rind removed, and diced
4 oz (100 g) onions, peeled and sliced
4 oz (100 g) potato, peeled and sliced
1 small lettuce heart, washed and finely shredded
2 pints (1.2 l) chicken stock
1 bouquet garni
1 lb (450 g) shelled peas
3 fl oz (75 ml) single cream
Salt and freshly ground black pepper
Croûtons

1. Melt the butter in a heavy-based pan, add the bacon and onions and cook gently for 3 to 4 minutes.

2. Add the potato and lettuce heart and cook for a further 4 minutes, then pour on the stock and add the bouquet garni.

3. Allow to simmer for 30 minutes or until the vegetables are thoroughly cooked.

4. Remove the bouquet garni and add the peas. Bring the soup to the boil and cook rapidly for about 5 minutes.

5. Purée the soup in a food processor or blender, then pass it through a fine sieve.

6. Add the cream and mix in well. Season to taste with salt and freshly ground black pepper and bring the soup slowly back to the boil. Serve immediately with a few croûtons scattered over the surface.

LOBSTER IN BRANDY
AND MEAUX MUSTARD SAUCE

This one is for the individual who feels that if they have to cook something then they're going to do it with style! You can purchase lobster already cooked and cleaned but do make sure that it is very fresh or properly defrosted and that you get the shell with it. If you are fortunate to have a friendly fishmonger, ask him to remove the flesh and cut it into fingernail-size pieces. Insist on him getting all of the flesh from the claws (this is where most of the meat is).

SERVES 1

1 cooked lobster, halved, flesh removed and the shell cleaned
2 oz (50 g) butter
2 oz (50 g) shallots, peeled and finely diced
1 clove garlic, peeled and crushed
1 teaspoon chopped parsley
1 tablespoon Meaux mustard
1 glass white wine
1 tablespoon brandy
5 fl oz (150 ml) double cream
Juice of ½ lemon
½ oz (15 g) Parmesan cheese, grated
Salt and freshly ground black pepper

1. Cut the lobster into fingernail-size pieces.

2. Melt the butter in a heavy-based pan, add the shallots, garlic and parsley and cook for 1 minute.

3. Add the mustard, white wine, brandy and boil for 30 seconds to reduce the liquid. Pour in the cream and lemon juice. Stir well and add the lobster meat and Parmesan cheese.

4. Bring the mixture to the boil, turn down the heat and simmer for 1 minute.

5. Season with salt and freshly ground black pepper.

6. Spoon the lobster into the shells and top with the sauce. Serve immediately with a glass of slightly chilled Puligny Montrachet and a green salad.

TUNA AND OLIVE BAKE
WITH CAPER MAYONNAISE

Not only tasty but also very healthy, these make an ideal main course or, if you prefer, scale down the recipe and serve as a hot hors d'oeuvre.

SERVES 4

8 oz (225 g) potatoes, peeled
½ oz (15 g) low-fat
  margarine
2 tablespoons milk
Salt and freshly ground
  black pepper
14 oz (400 g) tuna, flaked
2 tablespoons chopped
  fennel leaves
3 oz (75 g) olives, stoned
  and finely sliced
3 oz (75 g) shallots, peeled
  and finely diced
Grated zest and juice of ½
  lemon
1 oz (25 g) capers, chopped
1 tablespoon chopped
  parsley
5 fl oz (150 ml) mayonnaise
3 tablespoons plain flour
2 eggs, lightly beaten
4 oz (100 g) breadcrumbs
1 lemon, sliced

1. Boil the potatoes until cooked, drain and dry by placing back on the heat and stirring them continuously for a few minutes. Add the margarine and milk, season lightly with salt and freshly ground black pepper and gently mash them until smooth.

2. Once the potatoes are cool, mix in the tuna, fennel leaves, olives, shallots, lemon zest and check and adjust the seasoning if necessary. Place the mixture in the refrigerator and leave to chill for 30 minutes.

3. Add the chopped capers, parsley and lemon juice to the mayonnaise. Mix thoroughly, cover and keep cool until required.

4. Pre-heat the oven to gas mark 6, 400°F (200°C).

5. Mould the tuna and potato mixture into 8 round shapes. Dredge in the flour, shaking off any surplus, then the egg and finally the breadcrumbs.

6. Place on a lightly greased baking sheet and cook in the oven for 12 to 15 minutes.

7. Serve with the caper mayonnaise and garnish with lemon.

GRILLED LEMON SOLE
WITH CAFÉ DE PARIS BUTTER

Fresh fish, simply cooked, and spiced up with garlic and paprika – there's nothing nicer.

SERVES 1

1 lemon sole, cleaned and
 skinned
1 oz (25 g) plain flour
4 oz (100 g) butter, melted
Salt and freshly ground
 black pepper
Juice of ½ lemon
1 tablespoon chopped
 parsley
1 teaspoon paprika
½ clove garlic, peeled and
 crushed

1. Dry the sole with kitchen paper and dip both sides of the fish in the flour. Shake off the surplus and then dip the fish in the butter.

2. Place the sole on a grilling tray. Season with salt and freshly ground black pepper. Cook under a moderate grill for 10 to 12 minutes, turning very carefully during cooking.

3. Place the remaining butter in a pan over a moderate heat. Add the lemon juice, parsley, paprika and garlic and mix well.

4. Pour the sauce over the cooked fish.

POACHED EGGS BENEDICTINE

This dish, made famous by Sean Connery in one of the Bond movies, is one of my favourites. If you have never made Hollandaise sauce before – fear not. Simply take your time and be sure to add the butter gradually whilst continuously whisking and don't allow the sauce to overheat.

SERVES 4

2 tablespoons white wine vinegar
½ teaspoon black peppercorns, crushed
2 egg yolks
4 oz (100 g) unsalted clarified butter, melted
Salt and freshly ground black pepper
1 teaspoon lemon juice (optional)
4 eggs
1 tablespoon vinegar
2 muffins
4 slices tongue
1 teaspoon paprika
1 tablespoon chopped parsley

1. Place the vinegar and peppercorns in a saucepan and heat until the liquid has been reduced by two-thirds. Add the egg yolks and whisk over a pan of simmering water until the mixture becomes light.

2. Very gradually whisk the butter into the mixture, taking care not to let it separate.

3. Season to taste with salt and freshly ground black pepper and, if required, add a little freshly squeezed lemon juice. Cover and keep at a stable temperature, but do not overheat.

4. Gently poach the eggs in simmering water to which a little vinegar has been added.

5. Split the muffins and toast them. Place slices of tongue over the muffins, then lay the poached eggs on the tongue and cover with Hollandaise sauce.

6. Place them under a hot grill for a few seconds simply to glaze the sauce. Sprinkle some paprika and parsley over the top and eat immediately.

WARM ENGLISH CHEESE ON SPICY PARKIN WITH YOGHURT DRESSING

This dish is simplicity itself, although you could cheat if necessary and buy the parkin already made.

SERVES 4–6

4 oz (100 g) self-raising flour
4 oz (100 g) medium oatmeal
4 oz (100 g) soft light brown sugar
2 teaspoons ground ginger
1 egg, beaten
4 oz (100 g) black treacle
2 oz (50 g) butter
5 tablespoons milk
2 oz (50 g) English cheese per person, sliced ½ in (1 cm) thick
Lettuce leaves to garnish

For the yoghurt dressing:
4 fl oz (120 ml) plain yoghurt
1 oz (25 g) snipped chives
½ teaspoon paprika
Freshly ground black pepper

1. Pre-heat the oven to gas mark 4, 350°F (180°C). Line a 9-in (23-cm) square tin with greaseproof paper.

2. Place all the dry ingredients in a large bowl and beat in the egg. Warm the treacle, butter and milk together. Pour the dry ingredients into the warm syrup and mix well. Pour into the tin and bake for 45 to 50 minutes or until a toothpick inserted into the centre comes out clean.

3. Meanwhile, make the dressing. Combine the yoghurt and chives and mix in the paprika and freshly ground black pepper to taste.

4. When the parkin is baked, cut pieces that are the same shape as the cheese slices. Place a piece of cheese on top of each piece of parkin. Put on the grill rack and grill for 2 to 3 minutes until melted and lightly browned. Serve surrounded by the lettuce leaves tossed in the dressing.

Breast of Chicken in Paprika and Parsley Sauce

Most supermarkets now stock fresh plump ready-to-cook chicken breasts, also called 'supremes', and it is hard to imagine anything simpler to cook that is so pleasant to serve.

SERVES 4

4 chicken supremes
3 oz (75 g) butter
Salt and freshly ground
 black pepper
3 oz (75 g) shallots
1 red pepper, peeled,
 deseeded and diced
1 green pepper, peeled,
 deseeded and diced
1 tablespoon paprika
3 oz (75 g) tomatoes,
 skinned, deseeded and
 chopped
2 teaspoons chopped
 parsley
1 glass white wine
5 fl oz (150 ml) cream or
 plain yoghurt (whichever
 you prefer)

1. Lightly batter out the chicken supremes.

2. Melt the butter in a shallow, wide pan and, once hot, add the chicken. Season lightly with salt and freshly ground black pepper and cook thoroughly but gently (not too much colour).

3. Remove the chicken from the pan and keep it warm.

4. Add the shallots to the pan and cook for 1 minute. Add the red and green peppers and cook for a further 2 minutes.

5. Sprinkle on the paprika and add the chopped tomatoes and parsley. Mix well and add the wine. Simmer until reduced by half.

6. Pour in the cream or yoghurt, mix well and check the seasoning. Bring to the boil and pour over the chicken. This dish is lovely with pilaf rice and a salad.

═ BAKED POTATO WITH CHILLI CON CARNE ═

This is quite an adventurous recipe for the inexperienced cook. The simplicity of its preparation actually belies the taste and appearance of the finished dish.

SERVES 1

2 medium potatoes,
 scrubbed
Salt
2 oz (50 g) red kidney beans
1 tablespoon vegetable oil
2 oz (50 g) onion, peeled
 and finely diced
½ clove garlic, peeled and
 crushed
4 oz (100 g) minced beef
½ tablespoon plain flour
½ tablespoon tomato purée
4 oz (100 g) chopped
 tomatoes
5 fl oz (150 ml) beef stock,
 hot
½ teaspoon chilli powder
 or crushed dried chilli
1 small green pepper,
 deseeded and finely diced
Freshly ground black
 pepper

1. Pre-heat the oven to gas mark 6, 400°F (200°C).

2. Make an incision across the top of the potatoes. Sprinkle the base of a roasting tin with salt, add the potatoes and bake for 45 to 60 minutes until cooked.

3. Meanwhile, place the beans in a saucepan, cover with cold water, bring to the boil and boil for 15 minutes. Remove from the heat, allow the beans to soak for 1½ hours, then drain them.

4. In a separate pan, heat the oil, add the onion and garlic and cook gently for 3 minutes. Stir in the minced beef and cook until well sealed and all traces of blood and raw meat have gone.

5. Add the flour, mix well to absorb all the fat, and cook for 2 minutes. Add the tomato purée and chopped tomato, mix this in well, then gradually add the hot stock, stirring constantly.

6. Bring the mixture to the boil, turn down the heat to simmer and add the chilli powder, peppers and drained beans.

7. Turn down the oven to gas mark 4, 350°F (180°C). Season the mixture lightly with salt and freshly ground black pepper, cover with a lid and bake in the oven for 45 to 60 minutes.

8. Remove the tops from the potatoes and serve the chilli over surface.

Lemon and Apple Meringue Pie

The combination of these two fruits creates a really lovely taste sensation.

Serves 8

6 oz (175 g) plain flour
A pinch of salt
3 oz (75 g) butter
5½ oz (165 g) caster sugar
1 egg yolk
2 tablespoons iced water
Grated rind and juice of 2
  large lemons
7 oz (200 g) granulated
  sugar
10 oz (300 g) apples, peeled,
  cored and sliced
7 fl oz (200 ml) water
1½ oz (40 g) cornflour
2 large eggs, separated

1. Prepare the pastry by sifting the flour and salt into a large bowl. Rub in the butter, then add 1½ oz (40 g) of caster sugar and mix in.

2. Make a well in the centre and add the egg yolk and water and mix lightly to form a smooth dough.

3. Cover and place in the refrigerator for 1 hour. Remove 30 minutes before required and leave the dough to reach room temperature. Pre-heat the oven to gas mark 5, 375°F (190°C).

4. Use the pastry to line a lightly greased 8-in (20-cm) flan ring. Prick the base to ensure that the pastry remains flat and even. Cover with greaseproof paper. Fill with baking beans (not baked!) and cook in the oven for 15 minutes. Remove the beans and paper and bake for a further 5 to 8 minutes until golden brown. Remove from the flan ring and leave to cool on a wire rack.

5. Reduce the oven temperature to gas mark 2, 300°F (150°C).

6. Place the lemon rind, juice and granulated sugar in a deep saucepan. Add the apple slices and water. Bring to the boil and stir in the cornflour dissolved in a little water. Reduce the heat and simmer for 4 minutes, stirring to prevent the mixture from burning. Allow to cool.

7. Vigorously beat the 2 egg yolks into the mixture and then sieve this into the pastry case.

8. Whisk the egg whites until firm and then whisk in half the remaining caster sugar. Carefully fold in the remaining caster sugar and spread the meringue on top of the flan filling.

9. Bake until lightly browned. Serve cold.

SEMOLINA PUDDING WITH FRESH FRUIT BRUNOISE

It is so often the case that simplicity creates excellence. Semolina pudding, cooked correctly, is not only easy for the 'survivor' to produce but filling and tasty. The fruit adds some moisture and interest to the finished dish.

SERVES 4

1 pint (600 ml) milk
½ vanilla pod
4 oz (100 g) semolina
3 oz (75 g) sugar
1 apple
1 orange
1 pear
1 banana
3 fl oz (85 ml) apple juice
2 egg yolks

1. Pre-heat the oven to gas mark 3, 325°F (170°C).

2. Bring the milk to the boil with the vanilla pod, then remove the pod and discard.

3. Sprinkle in the semolina, add the sugar and stir thoroughly to ensure it is well mixed.

4. Transfer to a lightly greased ovenproof dish and bake in the oven for 25 to 30 minutes until cooked.

5. Prepare the fruit by peeling and cutting it into small cubes and soaking in the apple juice. Chill until required.

6. Remove the semolina from the oven and, using a fork, mix in the egg yolks. Serve with the fruit salad.

COMFORT CUISINE

When you and your body feel low, whether it is due to having just recovered from a viral infection, an excess of alcohol or simply that the world seems no longer to be your best friend, then it's time for a little comfort cuisine.

We all have our favourite culinary remedies. Mine happen to be lightly-boiled eggs and freshly-made celery soup (not at the same time, you understand). So perhaps if we understand just a little of the theory related to the role that vitamins and minerals play in this, it may help to determine the type of food that suits our needs best.

Vitamin B₁ (Thiamin)

Appetite loss, anxiety, personality changes, depression and nausea are all symptoms of a B_1 deficiency. The main sources of vitamin B_1 are meat, nuts, fish and wholegrains.

Vitamin B₆

This is essential in the metabolism of proteins so that the body can break down amino acids into usable substances. Alcohol can affect this vitamin adversely. Deficiency can lead to anxiety, depression, insomnia and can also cause dry or greasy facial skin. A diet which includes meat, fish, avocados, wholegrains, bananas and nuts will be of benefit.

Vitamin C

This is necessary for the repair of tissues and helps in the breakdown of excess cholesterol. Symptoms of deficiency include depression. Plenty of fresh fruit is the answer.

Magnesium

This is important for energy and sugar metabolism and an adequate supply will ensure that we retain healthy nerves and muscles. Symptoms related to deficiency include muscle cramps, nausea, mood changes, depression and a loss of appetite. The answer – plenty of green vegetables, wholegrains, almonds and brazil nuts.

Zinc

This helps to resist infection, assists in mental function and generally aids hormone production. Symptoms of deficiency include poor mental function, acne, eczema, and repeated infection. A diet which includes meat, wholegrains, nuts, peas, lentils and beans would be of value.

In general terms, comfort cuisine means to consider carefully the elements necessary to assist the body to stand up to the rigours of modern-day life. A little thought gives a lot of goodness! (So profound.)

═══ CHICKEN AND BROCCOLI SOUP ═══

When in need of a little gentle nourishment, I find chicken soup the perfect answer, and when enhanced with some magnesium (in the form of broccoli) it is better still. Straining the soup results in an easily digestible cream soup, although you can leave in the vegetables if you prefer.

SERVES 4

2 oz (50 g) butter
3 oz (75 g) onions, peeled
  and diced
4 oz (100 g) celery, diced
2 oz (50 g) leek, diced
3 oz (75 g) carrots, peeled
  and diced
6 oz (175 g) broccoli florets
1½ oz (40 g) plain flour
1¾ pints (1 litre) chicken
  stock
1 bouquet garni
Salt and freshly ground
  black pepper

1. Melt the butter, add the onions, celery, leek and carrots and cook for 2 minutes, stirring frequently.

2. Add the broccoli and flour, mix to form a roux and cook for 1 minute.

3. Add the stock gradually, then add the bouquet garni and season very lightly with salt and freshly ground black pepper.

4. Simmer for 35 minutes and then strain the soup. Check and adjust the seasoning if necessary.

5. If you feel well enough, add a little cream or yoghurt and serve a light cheese scone with the soup.

SOLE AND PRAWN MOUSSE

This is a light-textured mousse with a full flavour.

SERVES 4

8 lemon sole fillets,
  skinned
3 egg whites
5 fl oz (150 ml) whipping
  cream
Juice of ½ lemon
Salt and freshly ground
  black pepper
8 oz (225 g) cooked shelled
  prawns, minced
2 oz (50 g) butter
6 oz (175 g) carrots, peeled
  and shredded (use a food
  processor or mandolin)
4 oz (100 g) leeks, thinly
  sliced
4 oz (100 g) celery, thinly
  sliced
A pinch of fresh ginger

1. Pre-heat the oven to gas mark 4, 350°C (180°C).

2. Place the fillets between two sheets of wet greaseproof paper and gently flatten them.

3. Lightly grease 4 ramekins and line them with 2 of the fillets. Make sure that the skin side is inside.

4. Place 4 fillets into a food processor and mince them. Add the egg whites. Carefully add the cream and mix until smooth. Season with lemon juice, salt and freshly ground black pepper.

5. Add the prawn purée and fold in using a metal spoon. Divide the mixture into the ramekins and level the top.

6. Cut the remaining fillets in half and place the halves over the top of each dish.

7. Cover with lightly buttered kitchen foil and place in a roasting dish containing a little cold water.

8. Cook in the oven for 15 to 20 minutes.

9. Heat the butter in a large frying pan and add the vegetables. Season with ginger, salt and freshly ground black pepper. Cook for 2 minutes.

10. Turn out the mousse on to a plate and place the vegetables at random over and around the dish.

11. If your weight can take it, serve a Hollandaise sauce with this dish.

Delice of Sole Poached with Leeks in Lemon Sauce

The term 'delice' simply refers to a fillet which has been folded by drawing both the thick and thin end of the fillet over to cross the centre of the fish. This then allows you to place a filling neatly into the little nest created by this type of fold.

SERVES 4

6 oz (175 g) leeks
2 oz (50 g) butter
1 tablespoon vegetable oil
Salt and freshly ground
  black pepper
8 large lemon sole fillets,
  skinned
1 small onion, peeled and
  finely chopped
1 tablespoon chopped fresh
  fennel leaves
Grated zest and juice of 1
  lemon
5 fl oz (150 ml) dry white
  wine
2 tablespoons plain flour
2 fl oz (50 ml) double cream
A pinch of paprika

1. Pre-heat the oven to gas mark 4, 350°F (180°C).

2. Ensure that the leeks are thoroughly clean and cut them into very fine pieces of about 4 in (10 cm) in length.

3. Heat 1 oz (25 g) of butter and the oil in a pan, then add the leeks. Season with salt and freshly ground black pepper and cook gently for 4 to 5 minutes. Remove from the heat.

4. Lightly grease a shallow baking dish. Season the fillets lightly, then fold them as in the diagrams below left and transfer them on to the tray. Place an equal amount of the cooked leek in the centre of each delice (fillet).

5. Sprinkle the finely chopped onion and fennel around the fish. Sprinkle the lemon zest over the fish itself and add the lemon juice and wine. Cover with buttered greaseproof paper or kitchen foil and cook in the oven for 15 to 18 minutes.

6. Soften the remaining butter using a fork and add sufficient flour to make a smooth paste.

7. When the fish is cooked, transfer it to a warmed serving dish. Place the cooking liquid on a high heat and whisk in the butter and flour paste to form a sauce.

8. Add the cream, check and adjust the seasoning if necessary and pour over the fish. Dust lightly with paprika and serve.

EGGS BAKED WITH SPINACH

A classic dish which does much to make the soul feel better.

SERVES 4

8 oz (225 g) frozen spinach, thawed, or 1¾ lb (850 g) fresh spinach, cooked
A pinch of grated nutmeg
Salt and freshly ground black pepper
1½ oz (40 g) butter
1 oz (25 g) plain flour
10 fl oz (300 ml) milk
3 oz (75 g) Cheddar cheese, grated
2 fl oz (50 ml) cream
4 eggs

1. Pre-heat the oven to gas mark 6, 400°F (200°C).

2. Lightly grease a shallow baking dish and place the spinach over the base. Season with nutmeg, salt and freshly ground black pepper. Place in the oven and allow to heat through.

3. Melt the butter in a pan. Add the flour, mix well and cook for 1 minute. Gradually add the milk to form a smooth sauce. Add the grated cheese and season lightly with salt and freshly ground black pepper. Add the cream.

4. Rearrange the spinach in the dish so that it forms 4 nests, each with an indentation in the centre.

5. Break an egg into each nest. Season the eggs with a little salt.

6. Pour the sauce over the dish and bake in the oven for 10 to 15 minutes.

Welsh Rarebit

This savoury dish lends itself nicely to a night by the telly. You can regulate the strength of flavour by adjusting the amount of English mustard that you use. It tastes delicious with some spicy chutney.

SERVES 4

2 fl oz (50 ml) beer
1 oz (25 g) butter
1½ teaspoons plain flour
3 fl oz (75 ml) milk, hot
4 oz (100 g) Cheddar
  cheese, grated
1 egg yolk
1½ teaspoons English
  mustard (or more if you
  prefer)
Salt and freshly ground
  black pepper
4 slices bread
Butter for spreading on the
  toast

1. Bring the beer to the boil and boil until reduced by half.

2. Melt 1 oz (25 g) of butter in a heavy-based pan, add the flour and mix well. Cook on a gentle heat for 2 minutes. Gradually add the hot milk, stirring into a smooth sauce.

3. Add the grated cheese and allow the cheese to melt into the sauce, then remove from the heat. Add the egg yolk and beer and mix in thoroughly.

4. Season with mustard, salt and freshly ground black pepper and leave the mixture to cool. Meanwhile, toast the bread and butter it whilst it's hot. Spread the cheese mixture on the toast. Place back under the grill until golden brown.

Fresh Noodles Niçoise

There is something very rewarding about making your own pasta and this recipe ensures that you reap those rewards gastronomically.

SERVES 4

8 oz (225 g) plain flour
Salt and freshly ground
  black pepper
1 egg
4 egg yolks
2 tablespoons olive oil
2 oz (50 g) butter
2 oz (50 g) onion, peeled
  and finely chopped
1 clove garlic, peeled and
  crushed
8 oz (225 g) fresh or tinned
  tomatoes, chopped
1 teaspoon chopped parsley
1 oz (25 g) Parmesan or
  Cheddar cheese, finely
  grated

1. Sieve the flour and salt into a large bowl. Make a well in the centre and add the egg, egg yolks and oil. Mix to a smooth dough, cover with a damp cloth to prevent a skin from forming and set aside for 10 minutes.

2. Roll out the dough on a lightly floured surface until thin, then cut into 2 pieces, each 3 × 12 in (7.5 × 30 cm). Set aside for 3 hours in a cool place.

3. Cut the dough into ⅛-in (3-mm) wide strips. Cook in a large saucepan of lightly salted water for 12 to 15 minutes until just cooked. Drain well.

4. Melt the butter in a large saucepan, add the onion and garlic and cook for 2 minutes, then add the noodles, tomatoes and parsley, and cook for a further 2 to 3 minutes, gently lifting and moving the pasta with a fork.

5. Season to taste with salt and freshly ground black pepper. Serve at once in a heated earthenware dish or individual soup plates, sprinkled with a little grated cheese.

LASAGNE ALLA BOLOGNESE

*This dish can be made using plain white lasagne or lasagne verde,
flavoured with spinach. It can be made in advance and then re-heated.*

SERVES 4

2 tablespoons olive oil
3 oz (75 g) onions, peeled
  and finely diced
1 clove garlic, peeled and
  crushed
8 oz (225 g) very lean
  minced beef
1 oz (25 g) plain flour
1 × 14-oz (400-g) tin
  chopped tomatoes
1 tablespoon chopped
  parsley
1 heaped tablespoon
  tomato purée
1 glass red wine
4 fl oz (120 ml) beef stock,
  hot
1 bay leaf
Salt and freshly ground
  black pepper
6 oz (175 g) lasagne sheets
8 oz (225 g) Ricotta cheese,
  crumbled
4 oz (100 g) Mozzarella
  cheese, thinly sliced

1. Heat half the olive oil, add the onions and garlic and cook gently for 2 to 3 minutes. Add the beef and stir to ensure that it breaks up and gains even heat.

2. Sprinkle on the flour, mix it well so that any surplus fat is absorbed and cook gently for 2 to 3 minutes.

3. Add the chopped tomatoes, parsley and tomato purée and mix well. Cook over a medium heat for 1 minute. Pour in the wine, stock and bay leaf and season lightly with salt and freshly ground black pepper. Cook for 18 to 20 minutes over a low heat, stirring occasionally. Discard the bay leaf.

4. Meanwhile, bring a large pan of water to the boil and add the remaining olive oil (this will help prevent the pasta from sticking together). Add the lasagne a sheet at a time and boil for about 8 minutes or until the pasta is cooked.

5. Drain the lasagne and plunge it immediately into a bowl of cold water, a sheet at a time.

6. Pre-heat the oven to gas mark 4, 350°F (180°C) and lightly grease a 7 × 9½-in (18 × 24-cm) earthenware dish.

7. Layer some pasta over the bottom of the dish and place a little meat on top. Follow this with a light layer of Ricotta cheese and finally some Mozzarella slices.

8. Repeat the process until all the ingredients are used up. The final layer of

pasta should be topped only by the Mozzarella.

9. Bake in the oven for 30 to 35 minutes or until the cheese is melted and the lasagne is hot all the way through.

═ CHICKEN SAUTÉ IN LIGHT CREAM SAUCE ═

If you can't face the task of jointing the chicken, ask your butcher to do it for you. Many of the larger supermarkets now sell jointed chicken.

SERVES 4

3 oz (75 g) butter
1 × 3½-lb (1.5-kg) chicken, jointed into 8 pieces
2 oz (50 g) onion, peeled and finely chopped
4 oz (100 g) mushrooms, whole or quartered
2 oz (50 g) plain flour
1¾ pints (1 litre) chicken stock
Salt and freshly ground black pepper
1 egg yolk
1 tablespoon cream
1 tablespoon chopped parsley

1. Pre-heat the oven to gas mark 6, 400°F (200°C).

2. Melt the butter in a wide pan. Add the chicken pieces and fry until just coloured all over. Remove from the pan and put to one side.

3. Add the onion and mushrooms to the pan. Cook for 1 minute and then add the flour, mix well to form a roux and cook gently for 1 minute.

4. Gradually add the stock. Place the chicken pieces in the sauce and season lightly with salt and freshly ground black pepper.

5. Place in a casserole dish, cover with a lid and cook in the oven for about 20 to 25 minutes until the flesh is thoroughly cooked.

6. Mix together the egg yolk and cream. Add a little of the hot sauce and mix well. Then add the liaison of cream and egg to the chicken dish.

7. Check and adjust the seasoning if necessary and garnish with the parsley.

RICH RICE PUDDING WITH LEMON AND CINNAMON GLAZE

I enjoy a hot rice pudding with a spoonful of vanilla ice-cream and some chilled exotic fruits.

SERVES 4

1½ pints (900 ml) milk.
4 oz (100 g) short-grain rice
2 oz (50 g) butter
3 oz (75 g) caster sugar
3 eggs, beaten
Grated zest of 1 lemon
A pinch of cinnamon
5 fl oz (150 ml) double
  cream

1. Pre-heat the oven to gas mark 3, 325°F (160°C) and butter a 2-pint (1.2-litre) baking dish.

2. Place the milk in a saucepan, rain in the rice and slowly bring to the boil. Leave this to simmer, stirring occasionally, for 8 to 10 minutes.

3. Add the butter and sugar and remove from the heat. Leave this to cool for 5 minutes and then add a little of the mixture to the eggs (just to warm them slightly) and then add the eggs to the pudding and mix in thoroughly. Transfer the pudding to the prepared dish, sprinkle the lemon zest over the surface and sprinkle the cinnamon over the top.

4. Bake in the oven for 30 to 40 minutes and serve with cream.

BANANA OMELETTE

The two things that I find are of enormous help in making me feel better, both physically and spiritually, are omelettes and bananas, so I can find no reason why they should not be served together – after all, 'A little of what you fancy' and all that.

SERVES 2

2 bananas, peeled and
  sliced
1 teaspoon caster sugar
1 oz (25 g) butter
2 tablespoons double cream
  (use yoghurt if you prefer)
1 tablespoon runny honey
3 oz (75 g) unsalted butter
6 eggs, lightly beaten
1 oz (25 g) caster sugar

1. Sprinkle the bananas with the caster sugar.

2. Melt the 1 oz (25 g) of butter in a frying pan, then add the sliced bananas and cook over a medium heat for 2 minutes. Remove from the heat, and once they have cooled slightly add the cream or yoghurt and honey and mix well.

3. Melt the remaining butter in a reliable omelette pan. Once it is hot, but before it becomes brown, add half the egg mixture and cook over a high heat for about 2 minutes to make the first omelette. Spread the surface with half of the banana mixture, fold over and turn the omelette on to a serving plate, and keep in a warm place. Repeat the process to make the second omelette.

4. Sprinkle a little caster sugar over the top of each omelette, then place under a hot grill for a few seconds to glaze them. Serve immediately.

MONTH END CUISINE

Whether it be the end of the week or end of the month, dependent upon how the household budget is allocated, most of us encounter that age-old problem: how to provide good, healthy, nutritionally-balanced meals which are tasty, adventurous and yet kept within the limits of the budget available. Most of the less expensive food items tend to require slow methods of cooking (stewing, braising, etc.), but I feel that there is so much more flavour and taste from these cuts, especially where a dish is slowly cooked with vegetables in a rich stock, that this is by no means a disadvantage. The recipes in this section are written with economy in mind, but also aimed at providing high nutritional value and being substantial. In cases where the dish is cooked in the oven, try to plan your day to allow enough time to bake fresh bread, scones and so on, thus fully utilising the cost of using the oven.

CASSOULET

A very traditional dish, cassoulet is full of goodness, filling, yet economical.

SERVES 4

8 oz (225 g) white haricot
  beans
2½ pints (1.5 litres) water
4 oz (100 g) streaky bacon,
  rind removed and chopped
4 oz (100 g) garlic sausage,
  chopped (optional)
1 large onion, peeled and
  diced
½ bay leaf
2 juniper berries, crushed
1 clove garlic, peeled and
  crushed
1 tablespoon chopped
  rosemary
1 sprig of thyme
8 oz (225 g) boned shoulder
  lamb, fat free and diced
12 oz (350 g) belly pork,
  boned and diced
Salt and freshly ground
  black pepper
3 oz (75 g) fresh white
  breadcrumbs

1. Wash the beans thoroughly in at least 2 changes of water.

2. Place the beans and water in a saucepan, bring to the boil, then remove from the heat and leave them to soak for 2 hours.

3. Drain the beans and discard the water, then place them in a large flameproof pan with the bacon, garlic sausage, onion, bay leaf, juniper berries, garlic and herbs. Cover with 1¾ pints (1 litre) of water, bring to the boil and simmer for about 1½ hours.

4. Pre-heat the oven to gas mark 4, 350°F (180°C).

5. After 1 hour, place the lamb and pork in a roasting dish, season with salt and freshly ground black pepper and cook in the oven for about 30 minutes.

6. Once the beans are cooked, empty them into a colander placed over a saucepan to collect the liquid.

7. Place half the bean mixture back in the large pan. Drain the roast lamb and pork and add them to the pan, season lightly, then top up with the remaining bean mixture.

8. Pour on the retained cooking liquid and cover the top with the breadcrumbs.

9. Return to the oven and cook for about 1¼ hours.

GNOCCHI ROMAINE

This is ideal for adults and young children alike. If you prefer, use grated
Cheddar rather than Parmesan cheese.

SERVES 4

For the gnocchi:
1 pint (600 ml) milk
5 oz (150 g) semolina
2 oz (50 g) butter
1 egg yolk
A pinch of grated nutmeg
Salt and freshly ground
  black pepper

For the sauce:
1 tablespoon vegetable oil
2 oz (50 g) onion, peeled
  and finely chopped
1 clove garlic, peeled and
  crushed
A pinch of oregano
½ bay leaf
1 × 12-oz (350-g) tin of
  tomatoes, strained and
  chopped
1 tablespoon tomato purée
2–3 drops Worcestershire
  sauce
2 drops tabasco sauce
A pinch of sugar
2 oz (50 g) Parmesan
  cheese, grated

1. To prepare the gnocchi, bring the milk to the boil, then whisk in the semolina. Turn down the heat and slowly cook the semolina, stirring the mixture to prevent it sticking to the bottom of the pan. (It can be cooked in the oven if preferred.)

2. Once cooked, allow it to cool slightly, then add the butter, egg yolk, nutmeg, salt and freshly ground black pepper. Pour the mixture into a lightly greased shallow ovenproof dish and leave to go cold.

3. To make the sauce, heat the oil, add the onions and garlic and cook for 2 to 3 minutes until soft. Add the oregano, bay leaf and tomatoes, and stir frequently while allowing the sauce to cook for a further 2 minutes. Pour in any tomato juice left from straining the tomatoes and add the tomato purée. Season with Worcestershire sauce, tabasco sauce, sugar, salt and freshly ground black pepper. Remove the bay leaf and put the sauce to one side until required.

4. Pre-heat the oven to gas mark 4, 350°F (180°C).

5. Once the semolina is cold, turn it out on to a clean board which has been lightly sprinkled with semolina. Using a small scone cutter, cut the gnocchi into small rounds and put to one side. Place the gnocchi trimmings down the centre of the ovenproof dish and neatly lay the rounds of gnocchi over this.

6. Pour the sauce around the edge, sprinkle a little Parmesan cheese over the gnocchi and place in a hot oven for about 8 to 10 minutes to re-heat.

LEEK AND POTATO PIE

There is plenty of flavour and taste in this very down-to-earth, no-fuss recipe.

SERVES 4

2 lb (1 kg) potatoes, peeled and diced
1 egg
1 oz (25 g) butter or sunflower margarine
A pinch of grated nutmeg
1 tablespoon sunflower oil
1½ lb (750 g) leeks, sliced
8 oz (225 g) streaky bacon rashers, rind removed and chopped
Salt and freshly ground black pepper

For the sauce:
1½ (40 g) butter
1½ (40 g) plain flour
10 fl oz (300 ml) milk, hot
3 oz (75 g) red Leicester cheese, grated

1. Pre-heat the oven to gas mark 3, 325°F (160°C).

2. Place the potatoes in a large saucepan with water to cover. Bring to the boil, then reduce the heat to a simmer, cover and cook until tender. Drain well, then mash and beat in the egg, butter or margarine and nutmeg. Set aside to cool.

3. Heat the oil in a large frying pan. Add the leeks and bacon and season to taste with salt and freshly ground black pepper. Cook for 3 to 4 minutes, stirring occasionally. Transfer to an ovenproof dish and set aside to cool.

4. To make the sauce, melt the butter in a heavy-based saucepan. Add the flour, mix in well and cook for 2 to 3 minutes over a low heat. Gradually add the hot milk, stirring constantly, then add 2 oz (50 g) of the cheese and season to taste with salt and freshly ground black pepper.

5. Pour the sauce over the leek and bacon mixture and mix in well. Spread the potatoes over the top, fluff up with a fork and sprinkle with the remaining cheese. Cook in the oven for 15 to 20 minutes until golden brown. Serve at once.

RABBIT PIE

I much prefer a more solid type of pastry for this dish and so tend to use a suet base, but if your tastes are for a lighter touch, then use any crust that takes your fancy.

SERVES 4

12 oz (350 g) self-raising flour
6 oz (175 g) shredded suet
1 tablespoon chopped tarragon
Salt and freshly ground black pepper
3 tablespoons cold water
1 × 2½–3 lb (1.25–1.5 kg) rabbit, dressed and jointed
8 button onions, peeled and left whole
12 button mushrooms
6 oz (175 g) bacon, rind removed and diced
1 clove garlic, peeled and crushed
10 fl oz (300 ml) red wine
15 fl oz (450 ml) chicken stock
1 bouquet garni
4 oz (100 g) green peppers, deseeded and diced
6 oz (175 g) tomatoes, skinned, deseeded and diced
2 oz (50 g) plain flour
2 oz (50 g) butter

1. Mix the flour, suet and tarragon and season with salt and freshly ground black pepper. Add sufficient cold water to form a soft pastry. Cover with a cloth and place in the refrigerator until required.

2. Place the rabbit joints in a large saucepan, add the button onions, mushrooms, bacon and garlic to the pan. Season with salt and freshly ground black pepper and add the wine, stock and bouquet garni. Bring to the boil, cover with a tight-fitting lid and leave to cook gently for about 1 hour.

3. Pre-heat the oven to gas mark 7, 425°F (220°C).

4. Once cooked, transfer all the main ingredients into a casserole dish, leaving only the sauce. Discard the bouquet garni. Sprinkle the peppers and tomatoes over the rabbit mixture.

5. Bring the liquid to the boil. Meanwhile, mix together the flour and butter.

6. Add small pieces of the butter mixture (beurre manie being the posh name) to the liquid and whisk it in. This has the effect of thickening the liquid to a sauce consistency. Pour the sauce over the rabbit.

7. Remove the dough from the refrigerator and roll it out so that it is slightly wider than the top of the casserole dish.

8. Wet the edge of the casserole with a little water and top the dish with the pastry. Seal the edges using the thumb and forefinger.

9. Make three small incisions in the pastry to let any steam escape. Bake in the oven for 25 to 30 minutes.

═══════ CHUMP CHOP CHAMPVALLON ═══════

This makes a substantial meal using a cheap cut of lamb, slowly cooked with potatoes and onion in a light stock. You can radically alter the flavour of this dish by adding sliced vegetables, such as carrots, celery and leek to the recipe.

SERVES 4

2 tablespoons vegetable oil
4 × 4-oz (100-g) chump chops
Salt and freshly ground black pepper
4 oz (100 g) streaky bacon, rind removed and diced
1 lb (450 g) potatoes, peeled and sliced
8 oz (225 g) onions, peeled and sliced
4 large tomatoes, sliced
2 sprigs rosemary, finely chopped
15 fl oz (450 ml) chicken stock
2 oz (50 g) butter, melted

1. Pre-heat the oven to gas mark 6, 400°F (200°C).

2. Heat the oil in a wide frying pan. Add the chops, season with salt and freshly ground black pepper and lightly colour on both sides. Remove from the pan and place in a deep casserole dish.

3. Lightly cook the bacon pieces in the frying pan and add to the chops.

4. Cover the meat with a layer of sliced potatoes. Season lightly with salt and freshly ground black pepper and place a layer of sliced onions and tomatoes over them. Add the chopped rosemary and continue with layers of potato to finish the dish.

5. Pour in the stock and brush the top layer of potatoes with melted butter.

6. Bake in the oven for 45 to 60 minutes or until the top layer of potatoes is golden brown and the next layer is soft.

STUFFED CHICKEN LEG
IN RICH VEGETABLE SAUCE

By making extra sauce during the preparation of this dish, you will find you have a bowl of flavour-packed soup for the following day.

SERVES 4

4 chicken legs, boned
Salt and freshly ground
  black pepper
6 oz (175 g) sausagemeat
3 fl oz (85 ml) vegetable oil
4 oz (100 g) celery, sliced
3 oz (75 g) onions, peeled
  and diced
4 oz (100 g) leeks, sliced
4 oz (100 g) carrots, peeled
  and sliced
2 oz (50 g) plain flour
2 tablespoons tomato purée
2½ pints (1.5 litres) chicken
  stock, hot
1 bouquet garni

1. Pre-heat the oven to gas mark 6, 400°F (200°C).

2. Gently beat out the boned chicken legs, then season them lightly. Level the sausagemeat over the flesh, roll up like a swiss roll and secure with string.

3. Heat the oil and lightly colour the legs. Transfer to a deep casserole dish.

4. Add the vegetables to the hot oil and cook for 3 to 4 minutes. Stir in the flour until all the fat has been absorbed.

5. Add the tomato purée, then gradually add the stock. Once it is mixed in, add the bouquet garni and season lightly with salt and freshly ground black pepper.

6. Pour the sauce over the chicken, cover with a tight-fitting lid and cook in the oven for about 18 to 20 minutes. (It is essential to cook chicken thoroughly.)

7. Once cooked, remove the chicken from the dish and discard the string. Place on a clean warmed serving dish. Transfer the bulk of the vegetables to a serving dish, discarding the bouquet garni. Pass the sauce through a conical strainer. Check and adjust the seasoning if necessary.

8. Pour sufficient sauce over the chicken, then allow the remainder to cool before refrigerating to use later as a soup.

= BRAISED OXTAIL IN RED WINE WITH =
GLAZED SHALLOTS AND BUTTON MUSHROOMS

A 'get back to nature' dish that calls for a finger bowl with warm water and a clean napkin so you can comfortably pick the meat from the bones.

SERVES 4

2 fl oz (50 ml) vegetable oil
2½ lb (1.25 kg) oxtail, chopped
4 oz (100 g) bacon, rind removed and diced
4 oz (100 g) carrots, peeled and chopped
4 oz (100 g) onions, peeled and chopped
4 oz (100 g) leeks, sliced
4 oz (100 g) celery, chopped
1 clove garlic, peeled and crushed
2½ oz (65 g) plain flour
2 oz (50 g) tomato purée
1 large glass red wine
2¼ pints (1.25 litres) beef stock, hot
Salt and freshly ground black pepper
1 bouquet garni
2 oz (50 g) butter
8 oz (225 g) shallots, peeled and left whole
1 tablespoon chopped parsley
4 oz (100 g) button mushrooms

1. Pre-heat the oven to gas mark 6, 400°F (200°C). Heat the oil , then seal the oxtail on all sides. Transfer to a serving dish.

2. Add the bacon, vegetables and garlic to the hot oil and cook for 5 to 6 minutes, stirring continuously.

3. Add the flour and mix thoroughly, ensuring that all the oil has been absorbed. Continue cooking for 2 to 3 minutes, then stir in the tomato purée.

4. Gradually stir in the wine followed by the hot stock. Add the oxtail, season with salt and freshly ground black pepper and add the bouquet garni.

5. Cover with a tight-fitting lid and cook for 2½ to 3 hours.

6. Just before serving, heat the butter in a frying pan and cook the shallots and parsley for 3 to 4 minutes, add the mushrooms and cook for 2 minutes.

7. Adjust the seasoning and consistency of the sauce (see 8), strain over the oxtail and garnish with the shallots and mushrooms.

8. It is essential to check and adjust both seasoning and consistency of a dish which has undergone a lengthy cooking time. If it is too thin, boil the sauce to reduce slightly. If it is too thick, stir in a little more stock or wine and re-heat.

RAISIN PUDDING

An ideal 'filler' to satisfy young and old alike. This could quite easily become a family favourite.

SERVES 4

10 fl oz (300 ml) milk
Grated zest of ½ lemon
2 oz (50 g) cornflour,
   diluted in a little cold
   milk
A pinch of salt
1 oz (25 g) caster sugar
½ oz (15 g) butter
2 eggs, beaten
1 oz (25 g) raisins
1 oz (25 g) sultanas
6 tablespoons apricot jam
1 tablespoon water

1. Bring the milk to the boil and add the lemon juice. Gradually add the diluted cornflour, stirring continuously, and add the salt, sugar and butter.

2. Cook the mixture until it forms a dough (very much like choux pastry) and leaves the sides of the pan cleanly.

3. Remove from the heat and leave to cool for 10 minutes. Pre-heat the oven to gas mark 3, 325°F (160°C).

4. Gradually beat in the eggs until the mixture is very smooth. Add the raisins and sultanas and vigorously beat the mixture to ensure it is smooth and light.

5. Transfer the mixture into buttered and floured charlotte or soufflé moulds, filling them to two-thirds full, and sit the moulds in a deep tray containing cold water.

6. Bake in the oven for about 1 hour.

7. Place the apricot jam and water in a saucepan and bring to the boil. Mix well and sieve into a sauce boat.

8. Once the puddings are cooked, carefully remove them from the moulds and serve with the apricot sauce.

TREACLE TART

There is something very encouraging about a lovely treacle tart. At a time when finances are low, it costs so little money to make you feel like a king or queen – so luxurious.

SERVES 8
(ENOUGH FOR 2 DAYS)

12 oz (350 g) plain flour
A pinch of salt
6 oz (175 g) butter
3 eggs
2 tablespoons cold water
2 apples, peeled, cored and grated
5 oz (150 g) white breadcrumbs
5 tablespoons golden syrup
3 tablespoons black treacle
Grated zest and juice of 1 lemon
5 fl oz (150 ml) double cream
1 tablespoon milk

1. Make the pastry by sieving together the flour and salt. Add the butter and rub in to a sandy texture. Mix in 1 egg and add sufficient water to form a dough. Cover and refrigerate for at least 1 hour.

2. Pre-heat the oven to gas mark 6, 400°F (200°C).

3. Lightly grease a 10-in (25-cm) flan ring and line it with the pastry. (It's a good idea to allow the pastry to return to room temperature before attempting to roll it out.) Reserve a little of the pastry to lattice the flan.

4. Mix together the apples and breadcrumbs. Heat the syrup and treacle together to pouring consistency and add to the breadcrumb mixture. Add the lemon zest, juice, cream and eggs. Beat together until well mixed and pour into the flan dish.

5. Using the remaining pastry, decorate the top of the flan with a lattice design. Brush the pastry with a little milk and bake in the oven for 12 minutes, then lower the temperature to gas mark 4, 350°F (180°C) for a further 18 to 20 minutes.

QUEEN OF PUDDINGS

This is a pudding which, in my mind, sits alongside the best. A 'stand the test of time' sweet which can be equally well received at a formal dinner party or family luncheon.

SERVES 4

1 pint (600 ml) milk
4 oz (100 g) fresh white
 breadcrumbs
1 oz (25 g) butter
3 oz (75 g) caster sugar
Grated zest of 1 lemon
2 eggs, separated
Raspberry jam

1. Pre-heat the oven to gas mark 4, 350°F (180°C).

2. Heat the milk and add the breadcrumbs, butter, 1 oz (25 g) of sugar and the lemon zest. Allow to cool slightly.

3. Add the egg yolks, mix well and transfer the mixture to an ovenproof dish. Bake in the oven for 25 to 30 minutes until firm, then remove from the oven.

4. Heat the raspberry jam in a small pan and pour it over the surface of the pudding.

5. Place the egg whites in a clean mixing bowl and whisk until doubled in volume. Add 1 oz (25 g) of sugar and whisk in. Pipe this mixture over the pudding and sprinkle the remaining sugar over the surface. Bake for 10 minutes or until golden brown.

CREEP CUISINE

There are certain occasions in one's life when it may be necessary to entertain for reasons other than simply enjoying the company of friends. Perhaps a deal is important, or a promotion opportunity developing – the possibilities are endless. Therefore if there is more riding on the meal than the chance of a Michelin Star or a bunch of flowers, you may wish to spend a little longer on the planning stage. Ensure that you are provided with information on the guests' tastes, likes and dislikes, food allergies, whether they are vegetarian, if there is a religious background which affects your guests' dietary habits – in fact, the more information you can glean, the better. Once this is acquired, the next task is to marry what they like with what your household budget can afford and, finally, the level of skill you have to produce this gastronomic feast. For it is here that you can really fall down. It would be unwise to attempt an adventurous new recipe without having 'imposed' it on some willing family or friends for assessment purposes well in advance. Although, I have to confess, I prefer to treat all my guests as friends, irrespective of the nature of the occasion and, as the saying goes, 'cook from the heart'!

BAVAROIS OF SMOKED SALMON

This, to my mind, is a starter which always produces the desired result. A combination of smoked salmon, golden caviare and asparagus is pure genius.

SERVES 4

8 oz (225 g) smoked
  salmon, sliced
2 oz (50 g) smoked salmon,
  blended in a processor
Grated zest and juice of 1
  lemon
6 black peppercorns,
  crushed
4 parsley stalks
2 fl oz (50 ml) dry white
  wine
8 fl oz (250 ml) double
  cream
¼ oz (10 g) gelatine,
  dissolved in cold water
Salt and freshly ground
  black pepper
A pinch of cayenne pepper
4 teaspoons golden caviare
4 asparagus spears
5 fl oz (150 ml) plain
  yoghurt
1 tablespoon snipped
  chives
8 lemon segments
8 leaves dill

1. Lightly grease 4 ramekins with oil and line them with the sliced smoked salmon.

2. Place the processed smoked salmon in a large bowl set on ice.

3. Put half the lemon juice, the peppercorns, parsley stalks and wine into a pan and bring to the boil. Simmer until reduced by half, leave to cool for a few minutes and then add to the processed salmon. Mix well.

4. Gradually beat the cream into the mixture, taking care not to overbeat the cream. The consistency should be light yet firm.

5. Add the dissolved gelatine, mix well and season lightly with salt, freshly ground black pepper and cayenne.

6. Half fill the dishes with the mixture, then place a teaspoonful of caviare in the centre. Cover with the remaining mixture and place in the fridge to set.

7. Purée the asparagus in a processor, retaining the tips for garnish. Add the remaining lemon juice, the yoghurt and chives and season lightly with salt and freshly ground black pepper.

8. Flood 4 plates with the sauce and un-mould the bavarois into the centre.

9. Garnish with the asparagus tips, lemon segments, dill leaves and lemon zest.

A HOT SCALLOP MOUSSE
WITH SALMON CAVIARE SAUCE

This is a delightful dish and can be made using any flat white fish.

SERVES 6

14 oz (400 g) scallops
1 egg
1 egg white
2 fl oz (50 ml) double cream
Salt and freshly ground
  black pepper
1 tablespoon snipped
  chives
3 tablespoons water
3 tablespoons white wine
  vinegar
2 tablespoons shallots,
  finely chopped
8 oz (225 g) unsalted butter,
  at room temperature
1½ teaspoons lemon juice
2 tablespoons salmon
  caviare
12 leaves chervil

1. Purée the scallops in a food processor. Add the egg and egg white, process for 2 minutes, then chill for 40 minutes.

2. Pre-heat the oven to gas mark 6, 400°F (200°C).

3. Return the mixture to the food processor, add the cream and process for a few seconds only, until thick and creamy.

4. Season with salt and freshly ground black pepper. Add the snipped chives and mix lightly using a metal spoon.

5. Spoon the mixture into 6 lightly buttered dariole moulds, cover with kitchen foil and stand them in a shallow tray of water. Bake for 25 to 35 minutes.

6. To make the sauce, place the water, wine vinegar and shallots in a saucepan, and boil until reduced by two-thirds. Leave to cool slightly.

7. Gradually whisk in two-thirds of the butter, a small piece at a time. Return the sauce to a low heat, whisk harder and add the remaining butter.

8. Season with lemon juice and freshly ground black pepper and add the caviare. Do not re-boil.

9. Flood a little of the sauce on to the individual plates, turn out the mousses on the centre of the plates. Garnish with chervil and serve immediately.

LOBSTER RAVIOLI ON A FRICASSEE OF SHELLFISH

This is without question my all-time favourite recipe. But do be careful. Shellfish is stunning when fresh and handled correctly; devastating when not so fresh. So the rules are:
1. Buy live or cooked shellfish from reputable suppliers.
2. Prepare and eat the same day as purchase.
3. If re-heating pre-cooked shellfish, be sure to re-heat it thoroughly.
4. If in doubt – throw it out!
The first sign of a problem is a slightly ammoniac odour and a 'sticky' feel to the flesh.

SERVES 4

For the ravioli:
1 lb (450 g) fresh spinach, washed
1 lb (450 g) plain flour
Salt and freshly ground black pepper
3 small eggs, lightly beaten
1 tablespoon olive oil
1 oz (25 g) butter
1 oz (25 g) shallots, finely chopped
½ teaspoon chopped parsley
1 clove garlic, peeled and crushed
½ teaspoon French mustard
5 fl oz (150 ml) double cream
1 teaspoon grated Parmesan cheese
4 oz (100 g) cooked lobster flesh, shredded

1. Prepare the ravioli paste by cooking the spinach in a very small quantity of boiling salted water. Once cooked, drain and dry it by squeezing out as much water as possible. Purée the spinach in a food processor or liquidiser. Allow to cool slightly.

2. Sift the flour on to the spinach, season with salt and freshly ground black pepper and gradually beat in 2 of the eggs followed by the oil. Mix well to form a smooth dough. Cover and place in a refrigerator for 30 minutes.

3. Heat the butter in a saucepan, add the shallots, chopped parsley, garlic and French mustard. Cook for 2 minutes. Add the cream and Parmesan cheese. Bring to the boil and allow to reduce by half. Season with salt and freshly ground black pepper. Place to one side until required.

4. Remove the ravioli paste from the refrigerator and allow to reach room temperature.

**For the fricassee of
shellfish:**
2 oz (50 g) butter
2 oz (50 g) bacon, rind
removed and finely diced
2 oz (50 g) shallots, peeled
and finely diced
3 oz (75 g) leeks, finely
diced
2 oz (50 g) carrots, peeled
and finely diced
4 scallops, cleaned
4 oz (100 g) king prawns
2 oz (50 g) mussels, cleaned
3 oz (75 g) queen scallops
1 glass white wine
1 glass brandy
1 tablespoon French
mustard
10 fl oz (300 ml) double
cream
1 tablespoon chopped
parsley
2 oz (50 g) Parmesan
cheese, grated

5. Divide the dough in half and roll out the first half on a lightly floured table as thinly as possible into a 22 × 14-in (55 × 35-cm) rectangle. Do the same with the other half of the dough. Cover both rectangles with a damp cloth.

6. Add the lobster flesh to the cream sauce, mix well and place small spoonfuls of this mixture in rows 1 in (2.5 cm) apart on the first rectangle of dough.

7. Moisten the space between the filling with lightly beaten egg and place the other rectangle of dough over the first rectangle. Very carefully press down between the filled sections. Cut the ravioli using a pastry wheel.

8. Cook in boiling salted water for about 7 to 8 minutes.

9. For the fricassee of shellfish, melt the butter in a wide, heavy-based pan, add the bacon, shallots, leeks and carrots and cook for 3 minutes. Add the scallops and cook for 1 minute. Then add the prawns, mussels and queen scallops and cook for 1 minute.

10. Add the wine and brandy, boil to reduce by half and add the French mustard and cream. Bring to the boil, season with salt and freshly ground black pepper and add the parsley. Allow to simmer for 2 minutes.

11. Drain the ravioli. Arrange the fricassee on a large flameproof plate and scatter the ravioli amongst the dish. Sprinkle with Parmesan cheese and brown slightly under a hot grill.

Collops of Monkfish with Garlic and Tomato Confit on a Chervil-Scented Stock

I have raved for many years about the texture and flavour of this unfortunate-looking fish – and it wasn't so long ago that it also represented exceptional value for money. Alas, its increase in popularity has brought with it an increase in cost. But even considering this, I still feel it represents a good buy.

Serves 4

15 fl oz (450 ml) fish stock
3 tablespoons chopped chervil
Grated zest and juice of ½ lemon
2 oz (50 g) onion, peeled and diced
3 oz (75 g) carrots, peeled and sliced
½ bay leaf
1 lb (450 g) trimmed monkfish, cut into ½-in (1-cm) thick collops
Salt and freshly ground black pepper
2 oz (50 g) butter
4 cloves garlic, peeled and crushed
2 oz (50 g) shallots, peeled and finely diced
4 medium-size tomatoes, skinned, deseeded and chopped

1. Place the fish stock in a wide, shallow pan, add 2 tablespoons chervil, the lemon zest and juice, onion and carrots and bay leaf and simmer for 5 minutes.

2. Add the collops of monkfish and season lightly with salt and freshly ground black pepper. Cover with greaseproof paper and simmer gently until cooked.

3. Meanwhile, melt the butter in a pan, add the garlic and shallots and cook for 3 minutes. Add the chopped tomatoes and cook for a further 3 minutes. Season with salt and freshly ground black pepper.

4. Remove the fish from the stock and keep it warm. Bring the stock to the boil and reduce by one-third. Strain into a clean pan, add the remaining chervil, check and adjust the seasoning if necessary.

5. Place a spoonful of the tomato mixture on the centre of each plate. Lay the monkfish, slightly overlapping, around the outside and moisten the dish with the chervil stock.

TERRINE OF VEAL AND DUCK WITH BUTTER-GLAZED KUMQUATS

This is a lovely meaty terrine with an unusual twist by serving with hot kumquats, softened and seasoned with shallots, garlic and tarragon. The recipe works well when the quantities are increased thus enabling you to make enough to keep in the refrigerator for a family treat as and when required.

SERVES 8–10

8 rashers streaky bacon, rind removed
2 small onions, peeled and roughly chopped
1 lb (450 g) duck flesh, cut into strips
10 oz (275 g) veal, cut into strips
2 cloves garlic, peeled and crushed
2 teaspoons chopped parsley
2 teaspoons chopped tarragon
2 teaspoons chopped oregano
3 fl oz (85 ml) brandy
2 fl oz (50 ml) Cointreau
1 large egg
Salt and freshly ground black pepper
4 oz (100 g) butter
2 oz (50 g) shallots, peeled and finely chopped
½ clove garlic, peeled and crushed
1 teaspoon chopped tarragon
1 lb (450 g) kumquats, quartered

1. Line the base and sides of a small loaf tin with 5 slices of bacon.

2. Place the 3 rashers of bacon, the onions, duck and veal into a food processor and chop.

3. Add the garlic, herbs, brandy, Cointreau and egg, and season with salt and freshly ground black pepper. Transfer to the lined loaf tin. Sprinkle a little water over the surface and chill for 2 hours.

4. Pre-heat the oven to gas mark 3, 325°F (160°C).

5. Cover the tin with kitchen foil, place it in a roasting dish containing a little water and bake for about 1½ hours until the juice runs clear when a needle or thin knife is inserted in the centre.

6. Remove from the oven and place a baking sheet on the top of the pâté. Sit a heavy weight on the tray and leave to cool.

7. Once cold, turn it out of the tin and store covered in the fridge until required.

8. To prepare the kumquats, heat the butter and cook the shallots, garlic and tarragon for 1 minute, then add the kumquats. Cook for 5 minutes and serve hot with the pâté. Garnish with fancy salad leaves.

Fillet of Pork on a Bed of Lentils and Smoked Ham with Caramelised Apple

Lentils could be classed as one of the most underrated food items available to us. They lend a feeling of old-fashioned goodness to a dish whilst giving it a very sophisticated finish.

SERVES 4

4 × 6-oz (175-g) fillets of pork
4 oz (100 g) lean raw ham, minced in food processor
1 egg yolk
4 fl oz (120 ml) double cream
A pinch of cayenne pepper
Salt and freshly ground black pepper
1 tablespoon snipped chives
½ tablespoon vegetable oil
2 oz (50 g) smoked streaky bacon, rind removed and diced
2 oz (50 g) carrot, peeled and diced
1 medium onion, peeled and diced
2 oz celery, diced
3 oz (75 g) brown whole lentils, washed and drained
15 fl oz (450 ml) chicken stock
1 tablespoon chopped fresh oregano
2 oz (50 g) butter

1. Pre-heat the oven to gas mark 4, 350°F (180°C).

2. Make an incision in each piece of pork. Cover them with clingfilm or a sheet of plastic and lightly batter them out.

3. With the raw ham in the processor, add the egg yolk and process for 1 minute. Add the cream and mix until slightly thick. Season with cayenne, salt and freshly ground black pepper. Mix in the snipped chives. Place the mixture into a refrigerator for 30 minutes to chill.

4. Heat the oil in a heavy-based flameproof casserole. Add the bacon and cook for 4 minutes. Add the vegetables and cook for a further 5 minutes, stirring frequently.

5. Add the lentils, stock, oregano and season lightly with salt and freshly ground black pepper. Bring to the boil, cover and transfer to the oven. Cook for 40 to 45 minutes, stirring occasionally. Once cooked, check and adjust the seasoning if necessary. A little more stock may need to be added during cooking.

6. Remove the ham mixture from the refrigerator and spread it evenly over the pork fillets. Roll them up (like a swiss roll)

**4 fl oz (120 ml) white wine
cider**
**2 large eating apples, cored
and cut into 4 thick slices**
4 oz (100 g) demerara sugar
6 leaves chervil

and secure them either with string or
cocktail sticks.

7. Heat the butter in a flameproof
casserole dish and gently seal the pork
fillets, just lightly colouring them.

8. Add the wine cider and cover with a
lid. Cook in the oven for 35 to 40 minutes
until thoroughly cooked. Remove the
meat from the liquid and keep it warm.

9. Place the casserole on a high heat,
bring the liquid to the boil and add the
cream mixture. Boil to reduce the liquid
by half. Season to taste with salt and
freshly ground black pepper.

10. Cover the apple slices with the sugar
and caramelise either in the oven or under
the grill.

11. Shape the lentil mixture into 4 dariole
moulds and turn out on to the centre of 4
large plates.

12. Remove the string or cocktail sticks
from the pork, slice the meat into 4 thick
roundels and place around the outside of
the lentil pudding. Set the apple to one
side and just cover the meat with the
sauce. Arrange a few leaves of chervil on
the outer edges of the plates.

FILLET OF BEEF
WITH STILTON TARTS

There is something very sincere about the marriage of garlic and ginger infused into a prime piece of beef. I think it is the simplicity of the ingredients which produces such an honest flavour to the finished dish.

SERVES 4

1½ lb (750 g) beef fillet
4 cloves garlic, peeled and
  thickly sliced
2 oz (50 g) fresh ginger,
  peeled and thickly sliced
6 oz (175 g) butter
1 tablespoon vegetable oil
2 oz (50 g) celery, sliced
2 oz (50 g) carrot, peeled
  and sliced
2 oz (50 g) leek, sliced
salt and freshly ground
  black pepper
2 fl oz (50 ml) red wine
10 fl oz (300 ml) brown
  stock
3 oz (75 g) beansprouts
3 oz (75 g) mangetout,
  chopped
4 fl oz (120 ml) double
  cream
1 egg
3 oz (75 g) Stilton cheese,
  grated
A pinch of cayenne pepper
4 individual pastry cases,
  baked blind

1. Pre-heat the oven to gas mark 7, 425°F (220°C).

2. Make several incisions deep into the beef fillet and insert the garlic and ginger.

3. Heat 2 oz (50 g) of the butter with the oil in a roasting dish and place the beef in with the celery, carrot and leek. Season with salt and freshly ground black pepper. Cook in the oven for 20 minutes, or longer if you prefer.

4. Once cooked, remove the meat from the pan, strain off the surplus fat and then swill out the pan with the red wine and stock. Simmer until reduced by half, remove from the heat and beat in 2 oz (50 g) of butter. Strain into a sauceboat.

5. Melt the remaining butter in a wide-bottomed pan and add the beansprouts and mangetout. Season with salt and freshly ground black pepper.

6. Meanwhile, mix together the cream, egg, cheese and cayenne pepper and season with salt and freshly ground black pepper. Pour into the pastry cases and bake in the oven for 6 to 9 minutes.

7. Cut the meat into medallions, place a nest of beansprouts and mangetout on the centre of the plates. Set two pieces of meat over the nest with a tart to one side and a ribbon of sauce around the outside.

RASPBERRY SOUFFLÉS

Unadulterated heaven. This dish may be expensive, but it's capable of getting you the job.

SERVES 4

For the sauce:
10 apricots, halved and
  stoned
4 fl oz (120 ml) water
3 oz (75 g) caster sugar
1 vanilla pod
1 small glass brandy

For the soufflés:
4 oz (100 g) icing sugar
9 oz (250 g) raspberries
Juice of ¼ lemon
2 egg yolks
9 egg whites
A pinch of salt
½ oz (15 g) unsalted butter
1 oz (25 g) caster sugar

1. To make the sauce, place the apricots, water, sugar and vanilla pod in a pan, bring to the boil and simmer for 30 minutes.

2. Place 3 oz (75 g) of icing sugar, the raspberries and lemon juice in a food processor and blend until smooth.

3. Add the egg yolks and blend for 25 seconds.

4. Place the egg whites and salt in a large clean bowl and whisk until it nearly forms soft peaks (do not overwhip). Beat in the remaining icing sugar.

5. Add one-third of the egg whites to the raspberry mixture and then fold in the remaining egg white with a metal spoon.

6. Prepare the soufflé dishes by greasing them with the butter and sprinkling with caster sugar. Pre-heat the oven to gas mark 7, 425°F (220°C).

7. Fill the dishes to the top with the mixture and smooth the surfaces. Using a knife, gently ease the mixture away from the sides of the dish. This will allow the soufflés to rise more freely.

8. Place the soufflés in the oven and cook for 12 minutes.

9. Remove the vanilla pod from the sauce and purée or pass the sauce through a sieve.

10. Add the brandy to the sauce, and serve immediately with the soufflés.

CREAMED PEACHES WITH FRESH STRAWBERRY SAUCE

During the height of summer it is hard to imagine a more seasonal pudding than this, accompanied by a glass of very lightly chilled Muscat des Beaumes de Venise – Utopia! This recipe requires a substantial quantity of fruit, so search out slightly overripe peaches from the cheapest source. It is an expensive sweet but the flavour is sensational.

SERVES 4

12 peaches, skinned, stones removed and roughly chopped
6 oz (175 g) caster sugar
½ oz (15 g) gelatine
2 tablespoons kirsch
6 fl oz (175 ml) double cream, lightly whipped
4 strawberries, hulled and sliced
1 punnet strawberries (overripe will do fine)
4 mint leaves

1. Place the peaches with 2 oz (50 g) of caster sugar in a bowl, cover and refrigerate for 30 minutes.

2. Rub the fruit through a fine sieve and add a further 2 oz (50 g) of caster sugar.

3. Add 1 tablespoon of cold water to the gelatine then add a little hot water and mix well. Add this to the puréed fruit and stir until it has almost set. Pour in 1 tablespoon of kirsch, mix well and then, using a metal spoon, fold in the cream.

4. Half-fill the individual soufflé moulds and place a layer of sliced strawberries over the surface. Top up with the remaining peach mixture. Place in a refrigerator to set.

5. Purée the strawberries with the remaining caster sugar and kirsch.

6. Flood the serving plates with the strawberry sauce. Unmould the peach creams by dipping the moulds, to the brim, in hot water for a few seconds. Wipe away the moisture and turn upside-down on to the plates. Garnish with mint leaves and serve.

7. An alternative serving style would be to set the creams in brandy snap baskets (see following recipe).

Trilogy of Wild Mushrooms with
a White Butter Sauce

Passion Fruit Mousse Gently
Laced with Armagnac

Pilaf of Lambs' Kidneys with
Tomato and Basil

Scallop Fricassee with Warm Asparagus
and Chilled Oysters

Fillet of Beef with a Stilton Tart

Bavarois of Smoked Salmon

Treacle Tart

Breast of Chicken in Paprika
and Parsley Sauce

BRANDY SNAP BASKETS FILLED WITH WHISKY AND HONEY ICE-CREAM

I do think that a small ice-cream machine is a great investment in the home. Besides being great fun making your own weird and wonderful ice-creams, it is also extremely useful as you can always keep ready-to-serve home-made sweets in the freezer. That way you are never short of something nice to give unexpected guests when they arrive.

SERVES 4

5 oz (150 g) honey
10 fl oz (300 ml) milk, hot
2 egg yolks
5 fl oz (150 ml) double
 cream
1 glass whisky
4 fl oz (120 ml) golden
 syrup
3½ oz (90 g) butter
3 oz (75 g) sugar
1 teaspoon lemon juice
3 oz (75 g) plain flour
½ teaspoon ground ginger

1. Add the honey to the hot milk and bring the mixture to the boil.

2. Whisk the egg yolks in a bowl until nearly white, add the cream and whisk for 1 minute. Whisk in the boiling milk and honey, then add the whisky.

3. Strain the mixture through a fine sieve into a clean bowl and leave to cool. Transfer the mixture into an ice-cream machine and mix for about 20 minutes until the mixture sets. Place in the freezer.

4. Place the golden syrup, butter, sugar and lemon juice in a saucepan. Bring slowly to the boil, stirring. Remove from the heat and add the flour and ginger. Beat until smooth. Leave to become cold.

5. Pre-heat the oven to gas mark 6, 400°F (200°C).

6. Mould the mixture into small balls and press into circles on a greased baking tray. Bake in the oven for 5 to 10 minutes, then leave to cool for 2 minutes.

7. Remove from the tray using 2 palette knives and place each biscuit over a greased cup or mould. Allow to harden and become cold, remove from the mould and fill with the ice-cream.

SEDUCTION CUISINE

An intimate table for two is a standard setting for a romantic interlude. It goes without saying that the food for the occasion needs to be carefully planned and well executed. The obvious items which one might consider using include oysters and wild mushrooms – and there are many who would insist on including crushed rhino horn and ginseng. I must admit that I don't subscribe to that school of thought!

There are, however, certain foods which lend themselves to romance, and I would suggest scallops, asparagus, soft fruits and foods which are soft, gentle and require touching in order to eat them. Foods to avoid serving are heavy fatty items, highly-spiced pungent-flavoured dishes and excessively coarse-textured commodities (there is nothing romantic about watching your partner struggle through a tough piece of meat). But to a certain degree, food plays a secondary role to the organisation and setting. The selection of dishes should be such as to enable the host to enjoy the evening and not be tied to the 'stove' all evening. Much of the preparation should be done well in advance and the range of foods should vary and consist of light, easily-digestible items with interesting flavours and textures. Most important of all, remember to include some 'touching' food (items that need to be eaten with the fingers).

Finally, ensure that not only is the food ready, but also that the room and table are set for the type of occasion you have in mind and that you have left enough time to tidy yourself up, dust yourself off and relax, with sufficient energy left to enjoy the evening to the full.

TRELLIS OF SALMON AND SOLE WITH CHAMPAGNE SAUCE

This is a most delightful-looking dish with the trellis of pink salmon crossed with firm white flesh of lemon sole. It looks good enough to eat even before cooking!

SERVES 4

12 oz (350 g) fresh salmon, cut lengthways as for escalopes
12 oz (350 g) lemon sole fillets
4 sprigs dill
Salt and white pepper
3 tablespoons water
1 tablespoon vinegar
5 tablespoons Champagne (small bottle of *Babycham* even)
8 oz (225 g) unsalted butter, at room temperature
2 tablespoons snipped chives
Freshly ground black pepper
1 teaspoon lemon juice

1. Pre-heat the oven to gas mark 4, 350°F (180°C).

2. Cut the salmon and sole fillets into strips 4 in (10 cm) long × ¼ in (5 mm) wide.

3. Lay 3 strips of salmon on a clean surface and, using the strips of sole, intertwine to create a trellis effect.

4. Place the prepared fish on a sheet of lightly greased greaseproof paper. Place a sprig of dill on each one and season lightly with salt and freshly ground black pepper. Cover with a sheet of greased greaseproof paper.

5. Place on a baking sheet and cook in the oven for 10 to 15 minutes until cooked.

6. Put the water, vinegar and Champagne in a saucepan. Bring to the boil, reduce the heat and simmer for 6 minutes. Remove from the heat and allow to cool.

7. Add the butter in small pieces, whisking energetically.

8. Add the chives and season with salt, freshly ground black pepper and lemon juice. Do not re-boil.

9. Remove the fish from the oven. Carefully transfer it from the greaseproof paper on to warm plates and surround it with the sauce.

ROSETTES OF LAMB CAPPED WITH ONION MOUSSE

A rosette of lamb is simply a 2-in (6-cm) thick cut from the best end of lamb, neatly tied (like a fillet steak). Ask your butcher to prepare them.

SERVES 4

8 × 3-oz (75-g) rosettes of lamb
Salt and freshly ground black pepper
2 tablespoons vegetable oil
1 oz (25 g) butter
6 oz (175 g) onions, peeled and sliced
4 oz (100 g) patna rice
8 fl oz (250 ml) chicken stock
1 bouquet garni
2 egg yolks
4 fl oz (120 ml) double cream
1 tablespoon chopped rosemary

For the sauce:
2 oz (50 g) carrots, peeled and finely chopped
2 oz (50 g) onion, peeled and finely chopped
2 oz (50 g) celery, finely chopped
1 tablespoon plain flour
1 tablespoon tomato purée
1 tablespoon honey

1. Pre-heat the oven to gas mark 5, 375°F (190°C).

2. Lightly season the lamb with salt and freshly ground black pepper. Heat the vegetable oil in a wide shallow-bottomed pan and add the rosettes. Cook for 4 minutes on each side. Remove from the pan and place to one side. Reserve the fat.

3. Melt the butter in a saucepan, add the onions, cook for 1 minute and then add the rice. Cook for a further 1 minute, then pour in the stock. Bring to the boil, add the bouquet garni and season with salt and freshly ground black pepper. Cover with a lid and place in the oven for 16 to 20 minutes until the rice is cooked and the stock absorbed. Allow to cool.

4. Once the rice dish is cold, purée it in a food processor. Add the egg yolks and carefully beat in the cream until stiff enough to pipe. Season with salt, freshly ground black pepper and rosemary.

5. Place the lamb rosettes on a baking sheet and pipe a mound of the rice mixture on the top surface of the meat. Place them in the oven and cook for 12 to 15 minutes until golden brown.

6. Meanwhile, re-heat the pan containing the oil in which the lamb was sealed. Add the carrots, onion and celery. Cook for 3

10 fl oz (300 ml) chicken
stock, hot
12 sprigs of rosemary for
garnish

minutes, stirring frequently. Add the flour, mix to form a roux and cook for 2 minutes. Add the tomato purée and honey, mix well, then gradually add the hot stock. Bring to the boil and simmer for 5 to 8 minutes. Season to taste with salt and freshly ground black pepper.

7. Strain the sauce on to plates. Remove any string or cocktail sticks holding the meat into shape and arrange the meat on the plates. Garnish with rosemary.

BROCHETTE OF LANGOUSTINES ON A BED OF NOODLES

Just the mere appearance of this dish and you are talking seduction. There is no way that you can eat this without touching it.

SERVES 2

8 oz (225 g) cucumber
12 cooked langoustine tails
Salt and freshly ground
black pepper
3 oz (75 g) butter
1 oz (25 g) shallots, peeled
and finely chopped
1 clove garlic, peeled and
crushed
1 glass dry white wine
8 oz (225 g) tomatoes,
skinned, deseeded and
diced
1 oz (25 g) tomato purée
3 basil leaves, chopped
A pinch of sugar
2 fl oz (50 ml) vegetable oil
4 oz (100 g) noodles, cooked
and refreshed

1. Using a vegetable peeler or slicer, cut the cucumber into thin lengths about 3 in (7.5 cm) long.

2. Cover each langoustine with a slice of cucumber and thread them on to a skewer. Season lightly with salt and freshly ground black pepper. Place in the refrigerator until required.

3. Melt 2 oz (50 g) of the butter, add the shallots and garlic and cook for 1 minute. Add the wine, tomato flesh, tomato purée and basil leaves and cook for a further 5 minutes. Season with sugar, salt and freshly ground black pepper.

4. Heat the remaining butter with the oil and cook the langoustines.

5. Re-heat the noodles and place on a serving plate. Arrange the langoustines on top and coat with the sauce.

Veal Sweetbreads Braised in Marsala with Warm Brioche

The delicate flavour of this delightful gland is greatly enhanced by this particular recipe. If you have difficulties in obtaining veal, you could use lamb sweetbreads. Do allow two days when preparing this dish.

SERVES 4

2½ lb (1.25 kg) veal
  sweetbreads
4 oz (100 g) butter
10 oz (275 g) carrots, peeled
  and finely diced
10 oz (275 g) celery, finely
  diced
10 oz (275 g) onions, peeled
  and finely diced
6 oz (175 g) leeks, finely
  diced
1 bouquet garni
Salt and freshly ground
  black pepper
1 pint (600 ml) white wine
3 fl oz (75 ml) marsala
10 fl oz (300 ml) chicken
  stock
Brioche, thickly sliced

1. Place the sweetbreads in a bowl under running water for 3 hours.

2. Place them in a saucepan of fresh cold water, bring to the boil and simmer for 4 minutes. Refresh in cold running water and drain. Using the tip of a sharp knife, clean the sweetbreads by removing the membranes.

3. Cover them with a clean cloth and press them under a chopping board overnight. (This will ensure the excess moisture is removed.)

4. Pre-heat the oven to gas mark 5, 375°F (190°C).

5. Melt half the butter in a flameproof dish and add the diced vegetables, sweetbreads, bouquet garni and season with salt and freshly ground black pepper. Place in the oven for 6 to 8 minutes.

6. Add the wine, marsala and chicken stock. Bring to the boil and simmer for 5 minutes. Cover, return to the oven and cook for 15 minutes.

7. Remove the sweetbreads and vegetables from the liquid and keep them warm. Discard the bouquet garni.

8. Bring the liquid to the boil to reduce by one-third, then whisk in the remaining butter, cut into pieces. Do not re-boil.

9. Warm 4 slices of brioche (thickly cut) and place on large plates. Arrange the sweetbreads on the brioche, garnish with the diced vegetables and surround with the sauce.

SCALLOP FRICASSEE WITH WARM ASPARAGUS AND CHILLED OYSTERS

This has all the makings of a lovely evening, but do be careful to ensure that the shellfish is very, very fresh or any chance of romance will soon disappear. The rule I apply is 'If in doubt, throw it out' and head down to the local takeaway.

SERVES 2

4 oz (100 g) fresh asparagus, trimmed and pared
4 oysters
3 oz (75 g) butter
2 oz (50 g) shallots, peeled and finely chopped
6 oz (175 g) fresh scallops
1 teaspoon chopped parsley
2 oz (50 g) fennel, finely diced
Salt and freshly ground black pepper
1 glass white wine
2 tablespoons brandy
2 teaspoons French mustard
10 fl oz (300 ml) double cream or plain yoghurt
Selection of salad leaves such as frisée, oak leaf, etc.

1. Carefully cook the asparagus and keep it warm. Open and clean the oysters and place them immediately in the refrigerator.

2. Heat the butter in a wide frying pan, add the shallots and cook for 1 minute. Add the scallops, parsley and fennel. Season very lightly with salt and freshly ground black pepper and cook for 2 minutes, turning the scallops carefully.

3. Add the wine, brandy and mustard and cook for 1 minute, then pour in the cream or yoghurt and bring to the boil.

4. Check and adjust the seasoning to taste.

5. Arrange the salad leaves on a serving plate, place on the scallops and sauce and dress with the drained asparagus and chilled oysters.

═══ Warm Calves' Liver Salad with ═══ Lemon Mint and Pistachio Butter

*If you find it difficult to obtain calves' liver or would prefer not to use it,
then this recipe works just as well with ducks' liver or even very young
lambs' liver. The method involves dusting the liver with flour which
prevents it from becoming soggy once cooked. For it to be really effective,
the flour should be coated over the liver just before cooking it.*

SERVES 4

**Selection of fresh salad
  ingredients**
1 lb (450 g) calves' liver
**Salt and freshly ground
  black pepper**
1 oz (25 g) plain flour
**1½ tablespoons vegetable
  oil**
4 oz (100 g) clarified butter
**2 oz (50 g) shallots, peeled
  and finely diced**
**½ teaspoon black
  peppercorns, crushed**
**1 tablespoon chopped
  lemon mint**
**Grated zest and juice of ½
  lemon**
**1 oz (25 g) pistachio nuts,
  peeled and chopped**
**4 large tomatoes, skinned,
  deseeded and finely diced**

1. Prepare the salad ingredients and
arrange them on 4 large plates so that you
can sit the liver in the centre of the plates.
Place in a refrigerator until required.

2. Prepare the liver by removing any large
veins. Cut the liver lengthways into 4
slices. Season with salt and freshly ground
black pepper. Dip both sides of the liver
into the flour and lightly shake off any
surplus.

3. Heat the oil in a frying pan and, once
hot, add the liver. Cook for 2 to 3 minutes
on each side. Remove from the pan and
arrange on the prepared plates with salad.
Discard the oil from the frying pan and
place the pan back on the heat.

4. Add the clarified butter and, once hot,
add the chopped shallots and black
peppercorns. Cook for 1 minute and then
add the lemon mint, lemon zest and
pistachio nuts. Cook for 1 minute and add
the lemon juice.

5. Pour the butter over the liver, garnish
with a little of the diced tomatoes and
serve.

Passion Fruit Mousse
Gently Laced with Armagnac

A gentle, easy-to-eat mousse with a very romantic name.

SERVES 4

10 fl oz (300 ml) milk, hot
5 eggs
3 oz (75 g) caster sugar
8 passion fruits, shelled
½ oz (15 g) gelatine,
  dissolved in 1 tablespoon
  water
2 fl oz (50 ml) Armagnac or
  brandy
3 fl oz (75 ml) double
  cream, lightly whipped

1. Place the milk, 3 whole eggs, 2 egg yolks and the sugar in a large mixing bowl. Sit this over a pan of hot water and whisk until the mixture becomes thick.

2. Add 6 passion fruits, the dissolved gelatine and Armagnac or brandy to the mixture. Leave to cool.

3. Whisk the remaining egg whites until they form soft peaks and, using a metal spoon, fold them into the cooled mixture. Reserve a little cream for garnish and fold in the remainder.

4. Transfer to small soufflé dishes and refrigerate for at least 3 hours.

5. Serve either in the little dishes garnished with some whipped cream and a little passion fruit or be more adventurous and turn them out on to a plate. If you choose this method, dip the moulds in a little warm water for a few seconds, gently ease the pudding away from the sides of the mould and carefully tease them out.

Soufflé of Wild Strawberries with Black Pepper Sabayon

This is an extremely daring dish. The combination of a delicate soufflé, lightly flavoured with fresh strawberries, accompanied by an egg-based sauce highlighted with black pepper, is one that I think you'll find quite exciting. The recipe works well with any soft fruits.

SERVES 4

3 eggs, separated
8 oz (225 g) wild
  strawberries
8 oz (225 g) caster sugar
3 tablespoons water
1 oz (25 g) butter
1 oz (25 g) granulated sugar
2 oz (50 g) icing sugar
5 fl oz (150 ml) marsala
Freshly ground black
  pepper

1. Pre-heat the oven to gas mark 5, 375°F (190°C).

2. Whisk the egg whites until stiff.

3. Sieve the strawberries into a large bowl.

4. Place 6 oz (175 g) of caster sugar in a heavy-based pan with the water. Bring slowly to the boil and boil until it reaches 280°F (140°C).

5. Remove from the heat, add the fruit purée and mix in thoroughly.

6. Pour the hot purée in a stream on to the beaten egg whites and fold the mixture together using a metal spoon.

7. Lightly butter individual soufflé moulds and coat them with granulated sugar. Stand them on a baking sheet and fill them with fruit to three-quarters full.

8. Place the moulds on the bottom shelf of the oven for 2 minutes, then gently transfer them to the centre of the oven and leave to cook for a further 18 to 20 minutes.

9. Place the egg yolks, remaining caster sugar and marsala in a basin over a pan of boiling water. Whisk until the mixture has doubled in volume and become white and fluffy.

10. Season with freshly ground black pepper and divide the sauce into individual soufflé moulds. Cover until required.

11. Gently slide the tray containing the strawberry soufflés part of the way out of the oven and dust the top of each one with icing sugar. Place back in the oven for a few seconds, then repeat the process twice more.

12. Remove from the oven and place a strawberry soufflé and a mould of sabayon on individual plates to serve.

PAVLOVA WITH COINTREAU AND CHOCOLATE

There is something erotic about eating pavlova. I think it's because it's such a messy sweet.

SERVES 4

3 egg whites
A pinch of salt
7 oz (200 g) caster sugar
1 oz (25 g) cocoa powder
1 oz (25 g) granulated sugar
½ oz (15 g) cornflour
1 teaspoon lemon juice

For the topping:
Selection of fruit salad laced with Cointreau
7 fl oz (200 ml) double cream, lightly whipped

1. Pre-heat the oven to gas mark 1, 275°F (140°C).

2. Beat the egg whites and salt until stiff, then gradually add the caster sugar and continue beating for 6 minutes.

3. Mix the cocoa powder, granulated sugar and cornflour in a separate bowl. Add this to the meringue and stir in the lemon juice using a metal spoon.

4. Form the mixture into 4 small circles on a foil-lined baking tray. Bake in the oven for 2 hours. Turn off the heat and leave the pavlova to cool in the oven.

5. Mix the whipped cream with the fruit salad and place on top of each meringue. Chill before serving.

MANGO AND CINNAMON TARTS WITH BAY LEAF CUSTARD

This is an adaptation of the classic French 'tarte aux pommes' – a very thin, fairly crisp sweet, which in my opinion makes one of the loveliest puddings imaginable. The recipe makes enough for you to reminisce over a second helping served cold with clotted cream.

SERVES 6–8

8 oz (225 g) plain flour
A pinch of salt
4 oz (100 g) butter, cubed
  and softened
3 tablespoons water
1½ lb (750 g) mangoes,
  peeled and sliced
2 oz (50 g) granulated sugar
15 fl oz (450 ml) cream
2 bay leaves
4 egg yolks
1½ tablespoons caster
  sugar
1 teaspoon kirsch
3 tablespoons apricot jam,
  hot

1. Sift the flour and salt into a bowl and rub in the butter to a sandy texture. Add the water and knead to a smooth dough, roll into a ball, cover and refrigerate for 1 hour. Remove 30 minutes before required.

2. Pre-heat the oven to gas mark 4, 350°F (180°C).

3. Roll out the pastry into a thin sheet. Cut into 6-in (15-cm) diameter circles and place them on a greased baking sheet. Crimp the edges with your fingers to make a border and prick the bottom.

4. Lay the slices of mango, slightly overlapping, starting at the centre and working your way to the edge. Sprinkle with sugar and bake for 30 minutes.

6. Bring the cream and bay leaves to the boil in a saucepan. Mix the egg yolks, sugar and kirsch and pour the hot cream on to the mixture. Stir well, return to the pan on a low heat and stir until it thickens. Remove from the heat and discard the bay leaves.

7. Remove the cooked tarts from the oven and brush the surface lightly with jam.

8. Flood a little custard on to a plate, sit a tart in the centre and serve.

MOTHER-IN-LAW CUISINE

This could be a real daunting test – to cook for your loved one's mother. It's surprising just how every mother-in-law seems to be the best cook in the world. There's nothing for it other than to 'grab the bull by the horns', 'take hold of the dragon's tail' – or whatever expression you prefer to use – but essentially you must cook with confidence.

As with any occasion which is important to you and your partner, don't use this moment to experiment with an untried recipe. It's far better to play safe – use recipes that you know will work and include dishes which, from careful research, you know she will like.

SALMON FISH CAKES

Salmon has such a lovely distinctive flavour that dominates yet complements the other ingredients in this recipe. The recipe works well with any fish.

SERVES 4

12 oz (350 g) salmon, poached
12 oz (350 g) creamed potatoes
Grated zest of 1 lemon
Juice of ½ lemon
1 tablespoon chopped parsley
2 eggs
A pinch of cayenne pepper
1 oz (25 g) anchovies, finely chopped
1 tablespoon chopped mint
Salt and freshly ground black pepper
Flour for coating
Oil for frying

1. Mix together all the ingredients except the flour and oil in a large bowl. Season to taste with salt and freshly ground black pepper. If the mixture is warm then leave it to go cold.

2. Turn out the mixture on to a lightly floured board and divide into 4 or 8 equal-sized cakes (depending on how you wish to present them).

3. Pat them into round flat shapes and using the back of a knife mark the top of the cakes with a criss-cross pattern.

4. Heat a little oil in a large frying pan and shallow fry the fish cakes on both sides, patterned side in first, until golden brown. Remove from the pan and place on kitchen paper to drain before serving.

= GLAZED MUSSEL AND WATERCRESS SOUP =

The generous flavour of the mussels in this soup is given a new dimension by glazing the surface with creamed curry.

SERVES 4

2 lb(1 kg) mussels,
  scrubbed
4 shallots, peeled and sliced
3 sprigs of parsley
10 fl oz (300 ml) dry white
  wine
Salt and freshly ground
  black pepper
4 oz (100 g) butter
2 leeks, sliced
1 clove garlic, peeled and
  crushed
4 oz (100 g) onions, peeled
  and sliced
½ bay leaf
6 oz (175 g) potatoes, peeled
  and sliced
3 bunches of watercress
1 pint (600 ml) chicken
  stock
Juice ½ lemon
1 bouquet garni
6 fl oz (175 ml) milk
8 fl oz (250 ml) double
  cream
2 egg yolks
A pinch of curry powder
8 watercress leaves

1. Place the mussels in a large pan with the shallots, parsley and wine. Season lightly with salt and freshly ground black pepper, cover and bring to the boil. Simmer for 5 to 8 minutes, just enough time to allow the mussels to open. Discard any that haven't opened.

2. Strain the liquid through a strainer covered with muslin and remove the mussels from their shells. Allow to cool and refrigerate until required.

3. Melt the butter in a heavy-based pan and, once hot, add the leeks, garlic, onion and bay leaf. Cover and allow to cook without colouring until soft.

4. Add the potatoes and watercress. Cover with the chicken stock and mussel liquid. Add the lemon juice and bouquet garni and simmer for 30 minutes.

5. Remove the bay leaf and bouquet garni.

6. Pass the soup through a food processor, liquidiser or sieve and return it to the pan.

7. Add the milk and 5 fl oz (150 ml) of cream to adjust the consistency and season to taste with salt and freshly ground black pepper.

8. Gradually return the soup to the boil.

9. Lightly whisk the remaining cream with the egg yolks and curry powder.

10. Pour the soup into soup cups, add the

mussels and float the cream glaze over the surface. Place under a hot grill until browned and garnish with watercress.

STEAK, KIDNEY AND OYSTER MUSHROOM PUDDING

If I were rescued from being alone on a desert island for a year and were asked what would I like as my first meal back in civilisation, this would be it: the pinnacle of Great British cookery.

SERVES 4

12 oz (350 g) self-raising flour
6 oz (175 g) shredded suet
Salt and freshly ground black pepper
3–4 tablespoons cold water
1 lb (450 g) topside of beef, diced
8 oz (225 g) ox kidney, diced
2 tablespoons plain flour
4 oz (100 g) oyster mushrooms, diced
2 oz (50 g) onion, peeled and finely chopped
1 small clove garlic, peeled and crushed
A pinch of chopped tarragon
2 tomatoes, skinned and diced
5 fl oz (150 ml) beef stock
2 drops tabasco sauce
2 drops Worcestershire sauce

1. Prepare the suet pastry by mixing the self-raising flour with the suet, salt and freshly ground black pepper. Slowly add enough water to form a dough. Once ready it should feel like elastic and readily leave the bowl in one large ball.

2. Reserve enough dough for the lid, then roll out the remainder and use it to line a 2-pint (1.2-litre) pudding basin.

3. Toss the beef and kidney in the plain flour. Shake off the surplus and place them in a bowl. Add the mushrooms, onion, garlic, tarragon and diced tomato. Mix together and season with salt and freshly ground black pepper, then place in the pastry-lined basin.

4. Pour in sufficient beef stock barely to cover the ingredients. Add the tabasco and Worcestershire sauces.

5. Roll out the reserved pastry to make a lid. Wet the edges with cold water and place on top of the basin, nipping the paste together.

6. Cover with kitchen foil, allowing for the top of the pudding to rise slightly, and steam for 4½ to 5 hours.

Prawn and Tomato Pancake Glazed with Cheese Sauce

Pancakes – either savoury or sweet – are extremely versatile in that they readily accept whatever filling you wish to give them, are easily prepared, and act as a most substantial course on any menu. They are at their very best when eaten hot from the pan, but they do store and re-heat well, so they can be made in advance. If this is the case, you should layer the pancakes on top of one another, separated by pieces of greaseproof paper to prevent them from sticking together.

MAKES 12 PANCAKES

4 oz (100 g) plain flour
Salt and freshly ground
  black pepper
2 eggs
2 fl oz (50 ml) cold water
8 fl oz (250 ml) cold milk
1 tablespoon walnut oil
Grated zest of ½ lemon
1 tablespoon chopped
  parsley
3 oz (75 g) butter, melted

For the filling:
2 oz (50 g) butter
2 oz (50 g) shallots, peeled
  and finely chopped
1 clove garlic, peeled and
  crushed
4 oz (100 g) prawns, cooked
  and peeled
2 oz (50 g) mushrooms,
  finely sliced
4 large tomatoes, skinned
  and diced
2 fl oz (50 ml) white wine
1 pint (600 ml) cheese
  sauce
3 oz (75 g) butter, melted

1. Prepare the pancakes by sieving the flour and salt into a mixing bowl. Add the eggs and beat into the flour. Slowly whisk in the water followed by the milk. Whisk vigorously to remove any lumps, then season with salt and freshly ground black pepper. Add the walnut oil, lemon zest and parsley. Leave the batter to rest for 30 minutes in a refrigerator.

2. Meanwhile, prepare the filling. Heat the butter, add the chopped shallots and garlic and cook for 2 minutes.

3. Add the prawns, mushrooms and tomatoes and cook for 1 minute. Pour in the wine, bring to the boil and boil until reduced by half.

4. Add enough cheese sauce just to bind the prawn mixture together. Check and adjust the seasoning if necessary. Remove from the heat and cover until required.

5. Using a good pancake pan, heat the butter and cook the pancakes as thinly as possible. (Pancakes were never supposed to be copies of Michelin 2x radials!)

6. Once cooked, place the filling over half of each pancake and roll up.

1 oz (25 g) Parmesan
cheese, grated
1 tablespoon chopped
parsley
A pinch of paprika

7. Place the finished pancakes on a warmed flameproof serving dish and cover with the rest of the sauce. Sprinkle with Parmesan, brown under a hot grill and serve sprinkled with parsley and paprika.

═══ LAMB WITH SALPICON OF MANGO ═══ AND MUSHROOMS BAKED IN A PUFF PASTRY TRELLIS

Trellising the pastry over the lamb not only gives a lovely finished appearance to this dish but also makes for a much lighter main course than if it were completely covered.

SERVES 4

1 tablespoon vegetable oil
1 × 8-bone best end of
  lamb, boned
3 oz (75 g) butter
6 oz (175 g) mango, peeled
  and diced
4 oz (100 g) wild
  mushrooms
2 oz (50 g) onion, peeled
  and finely chopped
1 clove garlic, peeled and
  crushed
2 sprigs of rosemary
1 teaspoon crushed black
  peppercorns
1 glass red wine
Salt and freshly ground
  black pepper
8 oz (225 g) puff pastry
1 egg, beaten

1. Heat the oil and seal the lamb on both sides without colouring it. Remove from the pan and put to one side.

2. In a wide-bottomed pan, melt the butter and, once hot, add the mango, mushrooms, onion, garlic, rosemary and peppercorns. Cook for 2 minutes, then add the wine and simmer until reduced by half. Season lightly with salt.

3. Pre-heat the oven to gas mark 7, 425°F (220°C).

4. Roll out the pastry to twice the size of the lamb and brush the edges with egg.

5. Place the meat on one half of the pastry and run a lattice cutter over the other to within ¼ in (5 mm) of the edges.

6. Cover the meat with the mango mixture and bring the rest of the pastry over the mixture. Pin and trim the edges and brush with egg.

7. Bake in the oven for 20 to 30 minutes.

PEAR-CUSTARD PROFITEROLES WITH BRANDY CHOCOLATE SAUCE

Whatever these lovely little buns are filled with seems irrelevant – they are always a delight to serve and eat – but a combination of thick fresh custard, pears, chocolate and brandy is sheer heaven. It is advisable to make choux pastry as and when required. Once baked, profiteroles tend not to keep too well.

SERVES 4–6

3 fl oz (85 ml) water
2 fl oz (50 ml) milk
2½ oz (65 g) butter
½ oz (15 g) caster sugar
2½ oz (65 g) plain flour
2 eggs, beaten

For the custard and sauce:
2 comice or conference
  pears, very ripe
2 tablespoons brandy
10 fl oz (300 ml) milk
1 vanilla pod
3 oz (75 g) caster sugar
3 egg yolks
1½ tablespoons plain flour
½ tablespoon cornflour
½ oz (15 g) butter
8 oz (225 g) plain chocolate

1. Pre-heat the oven to gas mark 6, 400°F (200°C).

2. Heat the water and milk in a medium-sized pan and add the butter. Once the butter has melted and the water begins to boil, remove from the heat, add the sugar and gradually add the flour, beating it into the liquid. Continue beating energetically until the dough forms a clean ball and leaves the sides of the pan. Leave to cool slightly.

3. Beat the eggs gradually into the dough. Again, this requires a strong wrist and an enthusiastic approach.

4. Peel and dice the pears, place them in a basin and add the brandy.

5. Prepare the custard by bringing the milk to the boil with the vanilla pod. Leave to infuse for 5 minutes and then remove the vanilla pod.

6. Place the sugar and egg yolks together in a bowl and whisk until the mixture is thick and creamy. Add the flour and cornflour and whisk thoroughly.

7. Pour the milk on to the egg yolk mixture and then return the mixture to the cleaned pan.

8. Bring this slowly and lovingly to the boil, stirring continuously, and cook carefully for 4 minutes.

9. The sauce will thicken and some lumps may form. These should be beaten out with a wooden spoon.

10. Add the butter and mix in well. Pour the custard into a clean bowl and add the strained pears, cover with a damp piece of greaseproof paper. This will prevent a skin from forming. Allow to go cold.

11. Place small teaspoonfuls of the choux paste on to a lightly-greased baking sheet and bake in the oven for about 8 to 10 minutes. Increase the temperature to gas mark 7, 425°F (200°C) and bake for further 12 to 18 minutes. (This will give the profiteroles a lovely colour and ensure that they are crisp.)

12. Once baked, make an incision on the underside of each bun (this prevents them from becoming soggy and makes a little hole ready to take the filling) and place them on a wire rack. Leave to cool.

13. Make the chocolate sauce by melting the chocolate with the brandy from the pears in a small bowl set over a pan of hot water. Mix together to a sauce consistency.

14. Fill the buns from the underneath with the pear custard (you can do this easily by using a piping bag with a generous nozzle).

15. Pour the hot chocolate sauce on to dessert plates and arrange the profiteroles on the sauce.

═══ MICROWAVED TREACLE PUDDING ═══

This is where 'she who must be obeyed' has to bow down to modern technology versus traditional cookery. Here is a no-effort pudding ready to eat just 9 minutes after starting to make it – and no disputing the quality. Times refer to a 600+ watt oven.

SERVES 4

6 tablespoons black treacle
2 oz (50 g) butter
4 oz (100 g) soft brown
  sugar
2 eggs, lightly beaten
4 oz (100 g) self-raising
  flour
2–3 tablespoons milk

1. Place the treacle in a 2-pint (1.2-litre) pudding basin, and microwave on HIGH for 20 seconds to soften it. Tilt the basin so that the treacle covers the sides.

2. Place the butter in a mixing bowl and beat in the sugar, a little at a time, until the mixture becomes light and fluffy.

3. Gradually beat in the eggs until well blended. Fold in the flour and then add the milk, 1 tablespoon at a time, and mix well. The batter should be soft and smooth and should drop easily from a spoon.

4. Transfer the batter into the pudding basin and smooth the top.

5. Cook on HIGH, uncovered, for 6 minutes or until the pudding has risen and is quite firm.

6. Cover and leave to stand for 2 minutes, then check to ensure it is cooked by inserting a knife or trussing needle down the centre. The blade should be clean and free from batter when removed. If not, cook on HIGH for a further 1 minute.

7. Turn out on to a warmed serving dish (at this stage I would pour some double cream into a jug and roll my sleeves up!).

BOUND-TO-WORK SPONGE

The mum-in-law will quickly warm to you once she sees that your cakes are of the old-fashioned kind.

SERVES 4

4 oz (100 g) self-raising
  flour
1 teaspoon baking powder
4 oz (100 g) soft margarine
4 oz (100 g) caster sugar
2 large eggs
2 drops vanilla essence
2 oz (50 g) icing sugar
4 tablespoons jam
Whipped cream to taste

1. Pre-heat the oven to gas mark 3, 325°F (160°C).

2. Sift the flour and baking powder into a large mixing bowl. Add all the other ingredients (except the icing sugar, jam and whipped cream) and whisk. Once all of the ingredients are well blended, test the consistency by lifting a spoonful into the air, then tapping the spoon. If the mixture is perfect, it should drop easily from the spoon. If not, simply add 1 or 2 drops of cold water.

3. Divide the mixture between 2 lightly greased and greaseproof-lined 7-in (18-cm) sandwich tins.

4. Using a wet knife, smooth the surface and cook in the oven for 25 to 30 minutes.

5. Leave to cool slightly then turn out on to a wire cooling rack. Remove the paper and leave to cool.

6. Finish by spreading with jam and cream, then sandwich together and dust with icing sugar.

7. Make a huge pot of tea and put your feet up until the mother-in-law arrives!

WHOLEWHEAT BREAD

Tradition insists that the true test of a good home cook lies in the quality of the bread made by his or her own hands. I don't believe that it is too difficult to make bread, nor do I believe that the bread made in modern plant bakeries, handled from start to finish by machines, bears any resemblance to real home-baked bread. This simplified recipe and method for making wholewheat bread is fail-safe.

MAKES 2 × 1-LB (450-G) LOAVES

1 lb (450 g) wholewheat flour
A pinch of salt
10–14 fl oz (300–400 ml) water, hand-hot
2 teaspoons dried yeast
1 teaspoon sugar

1. Place the flour in a large mixing bowl, add the salt and mix in well. Warm the flour slightly by putting the bowl into an oven at gas mark 4, 350°F (180°C) for 5 minutes.

2. Meanwhile put 4 fl oz (120 ml) of the water into a small basin and add the yeast. Stir in the sugar, mix well and leave to stand for 10 minutes or until a good head has formed.

3. Make a well in the centre of the flour and pour in all the yeast. Using very clean fingers, draw the flour into the liquid whilst slowly adding the remainder of the water. Work the dough very hard to form a smooth surface.

4. Divide the dough in half and mould into rectangles to fit 5 × 3-in (13 × 7.5-cm) well greased loaf tins.

5. Place the dough in the tins and press it into the sides to ensure that the edges are lower than the centre.

6. Cover the tins with a damp clean cloth (this prevents a skin from forming), place in a warm area, such as a linen cupboard, and allow it to rise for about 45 minutes.

7. Pre-heat the oven to gas mark 6, 400°F (200°C).

8. Bake the loaves in the oven for about 30 to 35 minutes, then remove from the tins and turn upside down back in the tins. Bake for a further 5 to 8 minutes to crisp the base.

9. Check to see if the leaves are cooked by tapping the bottom of the loaves. This should give a hollow sound. Transfer to a wire rack to cool.

BREAD AND BUTTER PUDDING
WITH WHISKY AND HONEY CREAM

A super, rich pudding which is further enhanced by a dish of cream lightly whisked with honey and whisky.

SERVES 4

2 oz (50 g) caster sugar
3 eggs
1 pint (600 ml) single
  cream, hot
8 slices bread, crusts
  removed and buttered
1 oz (25 g) currants
1 oz (25 g) sultanas

For the honey cream:
5 fl oz (150 ml) double
  cream
1 tablespoon honey
2 tablespoons whisky

1. Pre-heat the oven to gas mark 4, 350°F (180°C).

2. Whisk the sugar and eggs together and add the hot single cream.

3. Cut the bread with a scone cutter to the diameter of ramekins.

4. Place a slice of bread on the bottom of each dish, sprinkle on half the currants and sultanas and half the custard. Finish by repeating the process.

5. Sit the dishes in a roasting tin of water and bake in the oven for 25 to 35 minutes.

6. Whisk the double cream with the honey and whisky until it forms soft peaks and divide between ramekins.

7. Serve the bread and butter pudding and cream in the ramekins on a large plate covered with a napkin and dressed with edible flowers.

OAT CUISINE

There have been great strides made in many restaurants across the UK to cater more adventurously for the vegetarian, and about time I hear you say! Yet it still amazes me to find many establishments whose contribution to this growing band of customers stretches no further than to an omelette or, at best, a nut cutlet. It would be fair to say that to cook vegetarian requires deeper consideration and pre-planning than to cook carnivore. The essential nutrients lost by excluding meat from one's diet need to be found from alternative sources, and it is possible to feel restricted with the range of foods available as substitutes. It is perhaps the fact that one is looking for a substitute that creates the problem, for there is no real substitute for meat, although some would argue that many soya products are virtually indistinguishable from the real thing. Perhaps the answer to successful vegetarianism lies within a philosophy of preparing foods to present as a meal in their own right and not as a substitute for something else.

So do be adventurous and use as wide a variety of ingredients as available. Adapt and adopt them to classic recipes and view each one as a gastronomic creation in its own right. Most important of all, be sure to give serious consideration to dietary needs by increasing the intake of carrots and leafy greens in order to compensate for the loss of fat-soluble vitamins A, D and E. Vitamin D can be taken in tablet form and vitamin E can be found in walnuts, hazelnuts, margarine and wholewheat flour. Beans are an excellent source of protein, especially soya beans, and so a diet rich in beans, milk, eggs for amino acids and brown rice for complex carbohydrates and fibre is essential.

Swiss cheeses are an excellent source for vitamin B_{12} which can also be found in milk and eggs and do remember to eat plenty of spinach, walnuts, wholegrain foods, milk and eggs in order to give the body sufficient iron.

Gazpacho Andaluz

I confess to being someone who, given a choice between cold soup or something else would opt for the latter. But I do consider this particular cold soup to be one of only a few exceptions to that rule.

SERVES 6

12 oz (350 g) tomatoes, skinned and deseeded

4 oz (100 g) white breadcrumbs, soaked in a little water

12 caraway seeds

3 cloves garlic, peeled and crushed

10 fl oz (300 ml) olive oil

2½ pints (1.5 litres) water

1 small cucumber, peeled and diced

1 red pepper, skinned and deseeded

10 fl oz (300 ml) mayonnaise

2 tablespoons vinegar

Salt and freshly ground black pepper

1. Mix the tomatoes and breadcrumbs in a food processor or blender, then add the caraway seeds and garlic. Mix well.

2. Add 1 pint (600 ml) of water and the oil, and leave the mixture to stand for 1 hour.

3. Add the remaining water, the cucumber, pepper and mayonnaise and blend.

4. Add the vinegar and season with salt and freshly ground black pepper.

5. Chill for at least 2 hours before serving.

SPANISH OMELETTE

You can almost feel the Spanish sunshine and smell the mimosa when cooking this authentic Spanish dish!

SERVES 4

3 fl oz (85 ml) vegetable oil
2 fl oz (50 ml) olive oil
1 medium-sized onion,
   peeled and sliced
2 large potatoes, peeled and
   sliced
1 red pepper, skinned,
   deseeded and sliced
1 green pepper, skinned,
   deseeded and sliced
4 eggs, beaten
Salt and freshly ground
   black pepper

1. Heat the oils and fry the onions and potatoes in a large frying pan. Be sure to turn them gently so that they do not burn.

2. Once cooked, remove them from the pan and retain the oil.

3. Mix the peppers, potatoes and onions with the beaten eggs and season lightly with salt and freshly ground black pepper.

4. Heat 2 tablespoons of the oil in a large frying pan and, once hot, add the egg mixture and cook until the sides are brown. Finish by placing the pan under the grill until the omelette is completely brown.

5. Remove from the pan and serve.

══ Mozzarella and Tomato Soufflé ══

A light yet substantial, tasty dish, this is ideal either as a snack or as a first course at a formal dinner party.

SERVES 4

3 oz (75 g) butter
1 oz (25 g) plain flour
5 fl oz (150 ml) milk, warm
½ teaspoon English
  mustard
A pinch of cayenne pepper
Salt and freshly ground
  black pepper
3 oz (75 g) Mozzarella
  cheese, finely chopped
1 oz (25 g) onion, peeled
  and finely chopped
½ clove garlic, peeled and
  crushed
4 large tomatoes, skinned,
  deseeded and diced
1 teaspoon chopped parsley
3 large eggs, separated

1. Melt 1 oz (25 g) of butter in a heavy-based saucepan, add the flour and cook carefully for 2 minutes.

2. Slowly stir in the milk to form a smooth thick sauce, and cook for 4 minutes.

3. Season with mustard, cayenne, salt and freshly ground black pepper. Remove from the heat and add the cheese, then leave to cool.

4. Pre-heat the oven to gas mark 5, 375°F (190°C).

5. Melt the remaining butter in a saucepan, add the onion and garlic and cook for 2 minutes. Add the tomato flesh, parsley, salt and freshly ground black pepper.

6. Add the egg yolks to the white sauce and mix thoroughly. Mix in the tomato mixture. Whisk the egg whites until they form firm peaks, then carefully fold them into the soufflé mixture.

7. Pour the mixture into 4 well greased individual soufflé moulds or 1 × 1½-pint (900-ml) well greased mould. Bake in the oven for 25 to 30 minutes until golden brown and well risen. The soufflé must be served and eaten immediately.

Spinach and Feta Pie

A really healthy recipe, this eats well when accompanied by a crisp salad, a few minted new potatoes and a glass of crisp, dry white wine. It's just as tasty served hot or cold.

SERVES 4

1 tablespoon olive oil
4 oz (100 g) onions, peeled and finely chopped
2 cloves garlic, peeled and crushed
3 lb (1.5 kg) fresh spinach, washed, trimmed and coarsely chopped
4 oz (100 g) mushrooms, sliced
1 tablespoon chopped chervil
1 tablespoon chopped basil
Freshly grated nutmeg to taste
Salt and freshly ground black pepper
4 oz (100 g) Mozzarella cheese, grated
4 oz (100 g) feta cheese, grated
2 oz (50 g) Parmesan cheese, grated
1 egg, lightly beaten
8 oz (225 g) filo pastry
3 oz (75 g) butter, melted
2 oz (50 g) soft white breadcrumbs

1. Heat the oil in a large saucepan, add the onions and garlic and cook gently until soft. Add the spinach and mushrooms and cook for 5 minutes only. Season very lightly with the chervil, basil, a little freshly grated nutmeg and salt and freshly ground black pepper.

2. Add the cheeses and egg and mix well.

3. Grease a 10-in (25-cm) shallow, round baking dish and pre-heat the oven to gas mark 4, 350°F (180°C).

4. Place a sheet of pastry on the tray, large enough for the edges to be able to fold over the filling once added. Brush any joins with melted butter. Sprinkle a light coating of breadcrumbs over the pastry, then add another 4 layers of pastry, sprinkling each one with breadcrumbs.

5. Spread the filling over half the pastry and fold the pastry over the top a layer at a time, lightly buttering each layer before folding the next one over. Seal the edges.

6. Bake in the oven for about 35 to 40 minutes until golden brown.

TRILOGY OF WILD MUSHROOMS WITH WHITE BUTTER SAUCE

Small parcels of filo pastry, tightly closed, encapsulate a depth of flavour from the mushrooms during cooking.

SERVES 4

6 oz (175 g) butter
2 oz (50 g) onion, peeled
  and chopped
1 clove garlic, peeled and
  crushed
8 oz (225 g) wild
  mushrooms, finely
  chopped
1 tablespoon snipped
  chives
1 tablespoon red wine
Salt and freshly ground
  black pepper
8 oz (225 g) filo pastry
1 glass white wine
4 fl oz (120 ml) double
  cream

1. Pre-heat the oven to gas mark 6, 400°F (200°C).

2. Melt 2 oz (50 g) of butter, add the onion, garlic, mushrooms, chives and red wine and season with salt and freshly ground black pepper. Cook for 2 minutes, then strain excess liquid into a pan and retain the mushrooms and liquid for later use.

3. Cut the filo pastry into 4-in (10-cm) squares. Melt 2 oz (50 g) of butter, brush the squares lightly with butter and place them in threes on top of each other.

4. Place spoonfuls of the mushroom mixture on to the centre of each top piece of filo. Bring all 4 edges to the top to form a little parcel and squeeze to secure. You could tie a little strip of leek around if you wish.

5. Bake the oven for a few minutes, just long enough to allow the pastry to cook.

6. Place the cooking liquor from the mushrooms over a medium heat, add the wine and bring to the boil. Add the cream and reduce the heat slightly, then simmer to reduce by one-third. Remove from the heat and slowly add the remaining butter.

7. Pour the sauce on to warmed serving plates, transfer the parcels to the plates and serve immediately.

RATATOUILLE NIÇOISE

On a dark, wet, miserable day there is nothing nicer than this dish to bring back memories or create an atmosphere of Provence.

SERVES 4

1 tablespoon olive oil
1 large onion, peeled and
  diced
3 cloves garlic, peeled and
  crushed
1 large aubergine, peeled
  and cut into ½-in (1-cm)
  cubes
3 courgettes, cut into ¼-in
  (5-mm) slices
2 green peppers, deseeded
  and cut into strips
2 red peppers, deseeded and
  cut into strips
6 large tomatoes, skinned,
  deseeded and chopped or 1
  × 14-oz (400-g) tin of
  tomatoes
1 tablespoon tomato purée
1 glass dry white wine
1 teaspoon marjoram
1 teaspoon basil
1 teaspoon oregano
A pinch of caster sugar
1 teaspoon Worcestershire
  sauce
3 drops tabasco sauce
Salt and freshly ground
  black pepper
4 oz (100 g) white
  breadcrumbs
1 tablespoon chopped
  parsley
8 black olives

1. Heat the oil in a large saucepan, add the onion, garlic and aubergine and cook for 1 minute. Add the courgettes, peppers and chopped tomatoes and cook for 3 to 4 minutes, stirring frequently.

2. Stir in the tomato purée and add the wine and herbs. Mix well and season with caster sugar, Worcestershire sauce, tabasco sauce, salt and freshly ground black pepper.

3. Cover with a lid and cook gently for 15 minutes. Once the aubergine is tender, remove the lid and allow the liquid to reduce so as to give the dish a 'stew'-like appearance.

4. Transfer the ratatouille to a large flameproof serving dish or 4 individual dishes, sprinkle the breadcrumbs on top and brown under the grill. Garnish with the parsley and olives.

VEGETABLE SHASHLIK ON A RICE PILLOW WITH TOMATO AND OREGANO SAUCE

There are no hard and fast rules as to the type of vegetable you can use for this recipe, but do remember to keep the size and shape as even as possible.

SERVES 4

1 aubergine
2 green peppers
1 red pepper
4 ripe tomatoes
8 button mushrooms
2 courgettes
8 okra
4 fl oz (120 ml) vegetable oil
2 oz (50 g) butter
4 oz (100 g) onions, peeled and finely chopped
2 cloves garlic, peeled and crushed
1 tablespoon chopped oregano
½ bay leaf
1 lb (450 g) tomatoes skinned, deseeded and chopped
1 tablespoon tomato purée
1 glass white wine
Salt and freshly ground black pepper
8 oz (225 g) basmati rice

1. Prepare the vegetables by cutting them into uniform-sized pieces. Leave the okra whole.

2. Arrange them attractively on kebab skewers and lightly brush them with the oil.

3. To make the sauce, heat the butter, add the onion, garlic, oregano and bay leaf and cook for 2 minutes.

4. Add the tomatoes, tomato purée and wine, season with salt and freshly ground black pepper and cook gently for 5 minutes.

5. Grill the kebabs, turning them frequently.

6. Cook the rice in boiling salted water until just tender. Drain well.

7. Place the hot rice on to a serving plate. Dress with the kebabs and pour the sauce over the vegetables, discarding the bay leaf.

GOULASH OF VEGETABLES

Meat is never missed in this dish because the delicious flavour is derived from the vegetables, tomato and paprika. Use whatever vegetables are good and economical.

SERVES 4

2 tablespoons vegetable oil
1 large onion, peeled and
  sliced
8 oz (225 g) carrots, peeled
  and sliced
1 red pepper, skinned,
  deseeded and cut into
  large chunks
1 green pepper skinned,
  deseeded and cut into
  large chunks
8 oz (225 g) courgettes,
  sliced
6 oz (175 g) cauliflower, cut
  into florets
6 oz (175 g) leeks, sliced
1 tablespoon paprika
1 tablespoon wholemeal
  flour
1 tablespoon tomato purée
1 × 14-oz (400-g) tin of
  chopped tomatoes
1 glass red wine
A pinch of cayenne pepper
Salt and freshly ground
  black pepper
2 drops tabasco sauce
5 fl oz (150 ml) vegetable
  stock, hot (optional)
4 fl oz (120 ml) soured
  cream

1. Pre-heat the oven to gas mark 4, 350°F (180°C).

2. Heat the oil in a large flameproof casserole dish, add the vegetables one after another, stirring frequently.

3. Dust with paprika, mix well and add the flour. Blend thoroughly to form a roux. Add the tomato purée, tomatoes and wine, and season very lightly with cayenne pepper, salt, freshly ground black pepper and tabasco sauce.

4. Cook in the oven for 25 to 35 minutes.

5. If necessary, thin the goulash down with the vegetable stock.

6. Serve accompanied by a sauce boat of soured cream and a dish of either gnocchi or rice.

MEAT-FREE SHEPHERD'S PIE

If I were to go vegetarian, I'm quite certain that I'd feel withdrawal symptoms because of an absence of shepherd's pie. This substantial recipe is not only a fair substitute, it is a lovely dish in its own right.

SERVES 4

5 oz (150 g) green lentils
5 oz (150 g) yellow split
  peas
1¼ pints (750 ml) vegetable
  stock or water
1 tablespoon vegetable oil
4 oz (100 g) onions, peeled
  and diced
1 clove garlic, peeled and
  crushed
4 oz (100 g) carrots, peeled
  and diced
2 oz (50 g) leek, diced
3 oz (75 g) celery, diced
A pinch of tarragon
Salt and freshly ground
  black pepper
1 tablespoon tomato purée
12 oz (350 g) tomatoes,
  skinned, deseeded and
  diced
1½ lb (750 g) potatoes,
  cooked and mashed
3 oz (75 g) butter
2 fl oz (50 ml) double cream
A pinch of grated nutmeg
2 egg yolks (optional)
4 oz (100 g) cheese, grated,
  to sprinkle on top

1. Wash the lentils and split peas, place them in a pan with the vegetable stock or water and bring to the boil. Cover and simmer gently for 45 to 60 minutes until they are soft.

2. Pre-heat the oven to gas mark 5, 350°F (180°C).

3. Heat the vegetable oil in a wide-based pan, add the onions, garlic, carrots, leeks and celery. Cook gently for 6 to 8 minutes. Season with tarragon, salt and freshly ground black pepper. Add the lentil and pea mixture to the softened vegetables and mix well. At the same time add the tomato purée and chopped tomato flesh.

4. Transfer the mixture to a large ovenproof dish.

5. Mix together the mashed potatoes, butter, cream and nutmeg and the egg yolks, if using. Season with salt and freshly ground black pepper. Pipe this over the surface of the filling and top with grated cheese.

6. Bake in the oven for 20 minutes until golden brown.

WALNUT CAKE
WITH BRANDY CAROB FILLING

This is the perfect accompaniment to a cup of tea. The advantage of using carob powder is that it has a lower fat content than cocoa powder and has more vitamins. There's plenty of goodness from the walnuts as well.

SERVES 4 BIG PORTIONS

3 eggs
3 oz (75 g) soft brown sugar
2½ oz (65 g) wholemeal flour
1 oz (25 g) carob powder
5 oz (150 g) carob bar
8 oz (225 g) low fat soft cheese
3 tablespoons icing sugar
1 tablespoon brandy
3 oz (75 g) walnuts, chopped
8 walnut halves to garnish

1. Pre-heat the oven to gas mark 5, 375°F (190°C).

2. Whisk the eggs and sugar in a bowl until the mixture is thick and creamy.

3. Sift the flour and carob powder, returning the bran from the sieve into the flour. Using a metal spoon, fold the flour into the egg mixture.

4. Lightly grease and line 2 × 7-in (18-cm) sandwich tins with buttered greaseproof paper and divide the cake mix between them.

5. Bake in the oven for 18 to 20 minutes until cooked. Remove from the tins and allow to cool on a wire tray. Remove the paper.

6. Place the carob in a basin set over a bowl of hot water and stir until melted. Remove from the heat and stir in the cheese and icing sugar then add the brandy and chopped nuts.

7. Cover the base of one sponge with two-thirds of the filling. Place the other sponge on top and cover the sides and top of the cake with the remaining filling.

8. Garnish with the walnut halves and serve.

SPORT CUISINE

Serious sportsmen and women are only too aware of the importance of diet in relation to performance, therefore for best results, food in this context must act not only to satisfy gastronomic needs, but also to ensure that sufficient fat, carbohydrate and protein are broken down to provide that all-important energy.

It is generally accepted that a diet high in carbohydrates is of value, and the best sources for this include flour, bread, bananas, lentils and beans. Unrefined starchy foods are preferable, as they are high in vitamins, minerals and fibre and low in fat, and therefore helpful in utilising the carbohydrate along with the protein.

The food should not be bulky and needs to be fairly light in protein, fat and dietary fibre, as these take time to digest. At this point, the importance of not eating too close to the time of an event should be stressed, as this can have a detrimental effect on performance. It results in the release of insulin, which impedes the utilisation of fatty acids and as such depletes unused glycogen more rapidly.

So a 'winning' diet needs to be carefully planned and could include a wide range of pulses, plenty of fresh fruit and vegetables, bread, dried fruits, low fat yoghurts, white fish and skinned poultry – oh, and a good pair of trainers!

LENTIL SOUP WITH CASHEWS

There is plenty of energy-producing goodness in this soup as well as some lovely flavour.

SERVES 4

2 tablespoons vegetable oil
1 tablespoon chopped
  coriander
1 onion, peeled and finely
  chopped
1 clove garlic, peeled and
  crushed
1 tablespoon tomato purée
6 oz (175 g) lentils
1¼ pints (750 ml) vegetable
  stock (chicken would do)
4 oz (100 g) carrots, peeled
  and chopped
2 leeks, chopped
4 oz (100 g) celery, sliced
2 oz (50 g) cashews,
  chopped
10 fl oz (300 ml) skimmed
  milk
1 bouquet garni
Salt and freshly ground
  black pepper
1 tablespoon chopped
  parsley

1. Heat the oil, add the coriander and onion and cook for 2 minutes. Add the garlic, tomato purée, lentils and stock. Bring to the boil and simmer for 5 minutes.

2. Add the vegetables and nuts and simmer for 25 minutes. Pour in the milk, add the bouquet garni and allow to cook very slowly for a further 30 minutes.

3. Remove the bouquet garni and purée the soup in a food processor or liquidiser. Season with salt and freshly ground black pepper.

4. Serve garnished with a little parsley.

CARROT AND CORIANDER SOUP

A bowl of goodness that not only helps keep you fit but also satisfies the inner man – how's that for gastronomic philosophy!

SERVES 4–6

1 lb (450 g) carrots, peeled
  and sliced
8 oz (225 g) potatoes, peeled
  and sliced
1 large onion, peeled and
  sliced
6 oz (175 g) leeks, sliced
2 oz (50 g) streaky bacon,
  rind removed and diced
8 crushed black
  peppercorns
1½ tablespoons crushed
  coriander
1 small clove garlic, peeled
  and crushed
1 bay leaf
2 pints (1.2 l) chicken stock
Salt and freshly ground
  black pepper
5 fl oz (150 ml) single
  cream

1. Place all the ingredients except the cream in a large saucepan. Bring to the boil, reduce the heat and simmer until the vegetables are cooked.

2. Remove and discard the bay leaf. Purée the soup in a blender or processor and return it to a clean saucepan.

3. Add the cream and bring back to the boil. Check and adjust the seasoning if necessary. Serve with a bowl of croûtons.

Poached Salmon with Carrot and Cucumber Spaghetti

This clean-tasting dish epitomises all that is good about summer for me. I like to accompany the dish with a few minted new potatoes and a crisp salad.

SERVES 4

5 fl oz (150 ml) dry white wine
5 fl oz (150 ml) water
2 oz (50 g) onion, peeled and sliced
2 oz (50 g) carrot, peeled and sliced
3 oz (75 g) leeks, sliced
2 parsley stalks
1 small bay leaf
4 × 6-oz (175-g) salmon steaks
Salt and freshly ground black pepper
8 oz (225 g) carrots, peeled and left whole
1 small cucumber, peeled
Juice of ½ lemon
5 oz (150 g) unsalted butter
1 lemon, cut for garnish
4 sprigs of dill or fennel

1. Place the wine, water, onion, sliced carrot and leek in a shallow, wide pan. Bring to the boil and add the parsley stalks and bay leaf. Reduce the heat and simmer for 8 minutes.

2. Sit the salmon steaks in the cooking liquid. Season lightly with salt and freshly ground black pepper. Cover and cook gently for a few minutes. Carefully turn the fish over and continue to cook until the centre bone is easily removed.

3. Meanwhile, using a mandolin or food processor, cut the carrot and cucumber into very thin long strips (resembling spaghetti). Cook both in boiling salted water until just cooked. Blanch in cold water and drain.

4. Remove the salmon and the vegetables from the pan, cover and keep moist and warm.

5. Increase the heat on the cooking liquid, add the lemon juice and allow the liquid to reduce by one-third. Dice 3 oz (75 g) of butter, remove the sauce from the heat and slowly add the diced butter, stirring constantly. Check and adjust the seasoning if necessary.

6. Melt the remaining butter, add the carrot and cucumber strips together and

re-heat. Season lightly and divide between 4 large plates.

7. Sit the salmon just to the side of the carrot and cucumber spaghetti and garnish the surface with the sliced vegetables from the cooking liquid.

8. Pour the sauce over the fish and garnish with lemon and dill or fennel.

CHICKEN SUPREMES IN MUSTARD AND MUSHROOM YOGHURT

This tasty, easy-to-prepare dish has an unusual 'sharp' flavour – and it's very good for you. Boneless breasts for this dish are available from most supermarkets.

SERVES 4

4 chicken supremes, skinned
2 oz (50 g) butter
Salt and freshly ground black pepper
2 oz (50 g) onion, peeled and finely chopped
2 oz (50 g) mushrooms, sliced
1 clove garlic, peeled and crushed
1 tablespoon chopped parsley
½ teaspoon chopped tarragon
2 teaspoons Dijon mustard
6 fl oz (175 ml) plain yoghurt
Juice of ½ lemon

1. Cut the breasts into ½-in (1-cm) slices taken from across the chicken breast.

2. Melt the butter in a large frying pan. Add the chicken pieces and season with salt and freshly ground black pepper. Once the chicken has been sealed on both sides, remove it from the pan and leave on one side.

3. Add the onion, mushrooms, garlic, parsley and tarragon to the pan and cook for 2 to 3 minutes. Add the mustard and yoghurt. Bring back to the boil and add the chicken collops. Simmer gently for a few minutes until the chicken is cooked.

4. Mix in the lemon juice and serve with rice.

CARBONNADE OF BEEF

'Beef cooked in beer' wouldn't sit well in the 'seduction' category – well, not for most people – but it is a most welcoming dish, with a lovely clean taste. This recipe follows the classical line in that it is finished off with cheese croûtons over the surface just before serving.

SERVES 4

1 tablespoon vegetable oil
8 × 3-oz (75-g) slices topside of beef (ask your butcher to slice this for you if necessary)
12 oz (350 g) onions, peeled and finely sliced
2 cloves garlic, peeled and crushed
5 fl oz (150 ml) beef stock
10 fl oz (300 ml) brown ale
1 bouquet garni
Salt and freshly ground black pepper
1 tablespoon cornflour, diluted with a little water
4 slices bread, crust removed, cut into triangles and fried golden brown
3 oz (75 g) Parmesan cheese, grated
1 tablespoon chopped parsley or chervil

1. Pre-heat the oven to gas mark 3, 325°F (160°C).

2. Heat the oil in a large frying pan. Add the slices of meat, season both sides lightly with salt and freshly ground black pepper and seal them. Transfer from the frying pan into a deep ovenproof dish.

3. Add the onions and garlic to the hot oil and cook for 2 to 3 minutes until soft and lightly coloured. Add these to the meat.

4. Keeping the temperature of the oil hot, add the brown stock and, using a wooden spoon, scrape any sediment from the base of the frying pan into the stock. Pour this over the meat. Add the beer, bouquet garni and season with salt and freshly ground black pepper.

5. Cover with a tight-fitting lid and cook in the oven for 1½ hours.

6. Remove and discard the bouquet garni and carefully pour the liquid into a saucepan, place over a high heat and bring to the boil. Stir in sufficient diluted cornflour to thicken the stock slightly and pour the sauce back over the meat.

7. Lay the fried croûtons on the surface of the dish, sprinkle the Parmesan over them and brown under a hot grill. Garnish with a little freshly chopped parsley or chervil.

MEDAILLONS OF BEEF WITH STUFFED AUBERGINE ON MUSHROOM AND CLARET SAUCE

This is a super combination – it has plenty of colour as well as taste.

SERVES 4

5 oz (150 g) butter
4 × 6-oz (175-g) fillet steaks
2 aubergines
2 oz (50 g) onion, peeled
  and finely chopped
1 red pepper, deseeded and
  finely chopped
1 green pepper, deseeded
  and finely chopped
2 tomatoes, skinned,
  deseeded and chopped
4 oz (100 g) mushrooms,
  sliced
1 clove garlic, peeled and
  crushed
1 glass red wine
Salt and freshly ground
  black pepper
4 sprigs of rosemary

1. Melt 3 oz (75 g) of butter, add the fillet steaks and season with salt and freshly ground black pepper. Cook to suit your own taste.

2. Cut the aubergines in half lengthways, remove the flesh and cut into dice. Retain the shells.

3. Melt the remaining butter and add the onion, peppers and aubergine flesh. Cook for 1 minute, then add the tomato flesh. Season with salt and freshly ground pepper. Cover and keep warm.

4. Remove the meat from the pan and put on one side. Add the mushrooms and garlic. Cook for 1 minute, then add the red wine and bring to the boil. Season to taste with salt and freshly ground black pepper.

5. Assemble the dish by filling the aubergine shells with the vegetable filling. Pour the sauce on to a main course plate. Cut the aubergine in half and place on the plate. Cut the steaks into two pieces and lay to the side of the aubergine halves.

6. Garnish with the rosemary and serve.

PILAF OF LAMBS' KIDNEYS WITH TOMATO AND BASIL

Lambs' kidneys are best when cooked very lightly, seasoned to perfection and eaten directly after being cooked. The rice dish is moist and full of flavour and together with the kidneys make for a lovely hot hors d'oeuvre or supper snack.

SERVES 4

3½ oz (90 g) butter
1 small onion, peeled and finely diced
1 clove garlic, peeled and crushed
1 tablespoon chopped basil
10 fl oz (300 ml) patna rice
1 pint (600 ml) chicken stock, hot
Salt and freshly ground black pepper
6 oz (175 g) lambs' kidneys, cored and diced
2 oz (50 g) shallots, peeled and finely diced
6 oz (175 g) tomatoes, skinned, deseeded and diced
1 glass dry white wine
1 tablespoon tomato purée
1 teaspoon Worcestershire sauce
2 drops tabasco sauce

1. Pre-heat the oven to gas mark 4, 350°F (180°C).

2. Melt 1 oz (25 g) of butter in a flameproof casserole, add the onion, garlic and basil and cook for 2 minutes. Add the rice and cook for a further 3 minutes, stirring frequently.

3. Pour the hot stock into the casserole and bring to the boil. Season lightly with salt and freshly ground black pepper. Cover with a lid and cook in the oven for 18 to 20 minutes or until all the stock has been absorbed by the rice.

4. Remove from the oven and stir in ½ oz (15 g) of butter, check and adjust the seasoning if necessary. Keep covered and warm.

5. Heat 2 oz (50 g) of butter in a shallow, wide-bottomed pan. Once hot, add the kidneys, season with salt and freshly ground black pepper and cook very quickly. Remove from the pan and keep warm.

6. Add the shallots, cook for 1 minute, followed by the chopped tomatoes to the pan. Cook for a further minute and then add the white wine. Allow to reduce slightly, mix in the tomato purée and

season with salt, pepper, Worcestershire sauce and tabasco sauce.

7. Assemble the dish by surrounding the kidneys, topped with sauce, with the rice and serve immediately.

MACARONI AND APPLE PUDDING

This is the stuff for carbo-loading. A real high-energy pudding which also packs a lot of taste.

SERVES 4

15 fl oz (450 ml) milk
3 oz (75 g) wholemeal macaroni
2 cooking apples, peeled, cored and diced
2 oz (50 g) sultanas
Grated zest of ½ lemon
Grated zest of ½ orange
1 oz (25 g) brown sugar
1 egg yolk
3 egg whites
2 oz (50 g) caster sugar

1. Pre-heat the oven to gas mark 4, 350°F (180°C).

2. Place the milk in a saucepan, slowly bring to the boil and add the macaroni. Simmer for 12 minutes, remove from the heat and add the apples, sultanas, lemon and orange zest and brown sugar. Mix well and add the egg yolk.

3. Whisk one egg white to double its volume and then, using a metal spoon, fold it into the macaroni mixture and transfer it to a flameproof dish. Bake in the oven for 20 to 30 minutes.

4. Whisk the remaining egg whites with the caster sugar until they form soft peaks. Pour over the surface of the pudding and brown under a hot grill.

Blackcurrant Muffins

Blackcurrants are an extremely rich source of vitamin C, although it has to be said that much of this will be lost whilst the muffins are cooking.

SERVES 4

4 oz (100 g) self-raising flour

4 oz (100 g) self-raising wholemeal flour

3 oz (75 g) light brown sugar

2 egg whites, lightly whisked

3 oz (75 g) blackcurrants, fresh (if using frozen, then defrost)

7 fl oz (200 ml) skimmed milk

2 tablespoons vegetable oil

1. Pre-heat the oven to gas mark 6, 400°F (200°C).

2. Place the flours and sugar together in a large bowl and mix well.

3. Add the egg whites and mix well, then add the remaining ingredients.

4. Transfer into 12 lightly-greased muffin tins and bake in the oven for 16 to 20 minutes until golden brown.

Soda Bread

An easy-to-make loaf which is aerated by the bicarbonate of soda and soured cream.

MAKES 2 LOAVES

**2 lb (900 g) wholewheat
flour
4 teaspoons salt
2 teaspoons bicarbonate of
soda
10 fl oz (300 ml) cold water
10 fl oz (300 ml) soured
cream**

1. Pre-heat the oven to gas mark 7, 425°F (220°C).

2. Mix together the flour, salt and bicarbonate of soda in a large bowl.

3. Mix the water and soured cream then gradually add to the flour, mixing to form a dough.

4. Divide the dough in half and knead them into the shape of a ball.

5. Place them on a lightly greased baking sheet and make an incision in the shape of a cross over the top surface of the dough.

6. Bake in the oven for about 25 to 30 minutes. Cool on a wire tray.

SPOIL YOURSELF CUISINE

Spoiling yourself is all to do with being indulgent, having what you want when you feel you need it most. This means different things to different people. For some, it involves a huge slice of cream cake, a heavily-buttered scone, a disgustingly-rich chocolate mousse, whilst for others, it's all to do with savoury items such as a plate of fresh shellfish cooked with a little garlic and lemon, just seconds before you sit down in front of a roaring fire with a large glass of chilled white wine – heaven! But whatever the choice, it's usually the case that you feel you have deserved the moment. So here are ten 'spoil yourself dishes' which are easy to prepare and capable of giving you a little pleasure, relaxation and feeling of fulfilment.

CROQUE MONSIEUR

This hot cheese and ham sandwich is a real treat when accompanied by a crisp green salad and a glass of wine.

SERVES 4

8 slices white bread, crusts removed
4 oz (500 g) butter
8 slices Gruyère cheese
4 thin slices ham
2 tablespoons oil

1. Butter the bread using half the butter, then place slices of cheese on 4 slices of bread, lay slices of ham on the cheese, top them with another slice of cheese and top with another slice of buttered bread, making 4 sandwiches.

2. Using a round cutter, calculate the best way of cutting through the sandwiches in order to get the maximum number from each one.

3. Melt the remaining butter with the oil in a large frying pan. Once hot, add the sandwiches and cook carefully on both sides for 2 to 3 minutes until golden brown.

BAKED AVOCADO

This dish is easy to make and interesting to eat. Be sure to select avocados which are ripe, or leave enough time for them to ripen. Seasoning is particularly important in this dish, as it is in all avocado dishes, due to the blandness of the fruit.

SERVES 4

2 oz (50 g) cooked ham, chopped
2 oz (50 g) tomatoes, skinned, deseeded and chopped
4 oz (100 g) peeled prawns
Juice of 1 lemon
4 fl oz (120 ml) mayonnaise
Salt and freshly ground black pepper
2 avocado pears
2 oz (50 g) Parmesan cheese, grated

1. Pre-heat the oven to gas mark 6, 400°F (200°C).

2. Mix together the ham, tomatoes, prawns, lemon juice and mayonnaise. Season with salt and freshly ground black pepper.

3. Cut the avocados in half and remove the stones. Take the flesh out of the shells taking care not to damage the shells. Chop the flesh and add to the mayonnaise mixture.

4. Pile the filling back into the shells and sprinkle with Parmesan. Place in an ovenproof dish and bake in the oven for 10 minutes.

Butter-Fried King Prawns in Chive and Lemon Hollandaise

The hollandaise sauce can be made in advance for this dish, then covered and kept in a cool place, but be sure to use good, fresh eggs and use the sauce within 4 hours of making it.

SERVES 4

For the sauce:
2 tablespoons white wine
  vinegar
5 tablespoons water
8 black peppercorns,
  crushed
2 teaspoons chopped
  parsley
4 egg yolks
Salt and freshly ground
  black pepper
8 oz (225 g) unsalted butter,
  melted and strained
2 tablespoons snipped
  chives

For the prawns:
8 oz (225 g) butter
12 oz (350 g) king prawns
2 cloves garlic, peeled and
  crushed
Juice of 1 lemon
2 tablespoons snipped
  chives
1 lemon, sliced
4 sprigs of dill or parsley

1. To prepare sauce, place the wine vinegar, 4 tablespoons of water, the crushed black peppercorns and chopped parsley in a pan and boil until reduced by half.

2. Place the reduced liquid in a mixing bowl, add the remaining water and the egg yolks, season lightly with salt and freshly ground black pepper and whisk over a pan of warm water.

3. Gradually add the unsalted butter, whisking constantly.

4. Once all the butter has been added, keep whisking for 2 minutes. Add the chives, season with salt and freshly ground black pepper. Remove from the heat and put to one side.

5. To prepare the prawns, melt the butter and, once hot, add the king prawns, garlic, lemon juice and chives and season with freshly ground black pepper. Heat carefully until cooked.

6. Pile the prawns on a serving dish and pour over the hollandaise sauce. Garnish with the lemon slices and a little dill or parsley and serve with a rice dish.

SCRAMBLED EGG WITH JULIENNE OF SMOKED SALMON

Scrambled eggs is a dish which I consider it a sin not to eat the second that it leaves the pan. This recipe produces a 'wet' scrambled egg which is best eaten using a spoon and fork.

SERVES 4

1 oz (25 g) butter
8 medium eggs, lightly
  beaten
4 oz (100 g) smoked
  salmon, cut into long thin
  strips (the thinner the
  better)
Grated zest of ½ lemon
1 tablespoon snipped
  chives
Salt and freshly ground
  black pepper
5 tablespoons double cream

1. Melt the butter in the top of a double boiler over hot water.

2. Pour the eggs into the butter, then add the smoked salmon, lemon zest and chives and season with salt and freshly ground black pepper. Stir with a wooden spoon until the mixture becomes thick and creamy.

3. Gradually add the cream and remove from the heat. Check and adjust the seasoning if necessary and serve immediately.

BLACK PUDDING WITH DIJON MUSTARD SAUCE

*Often used as an integral part of the Englishman's breakfast, this dish
makes a lovely starter or is ideal just as a snack on its own.*

SERVES 4

3 oz (75 g) butter
2 tablespoons lemon juice
2 egg yolks
1 tablespoon white wine
1 tablespoon Dijon
  mustard (or more if you
  prefer)
1 tablespoon chopped
  parsley
Salt and freshly ground
  black pepper
1 lb (450 g) black pudding
1 medium onion, peeled
  and finely diced

1. Place 2 oz (50 g) of butter, cut into
pieces, the lemon juice, egg yolks and
wine in a pan. Sit this in a double boiler
over hot water and whisk until the
mixture thickens.

2. Transfer into a clean basin and leave to
cool. Once cool, add the mustard and
parsley. Season with salt and freshly
ground black pepper.

3. Cut the black pudding into roundels
about 1 in (2.5 cm) thick. Melt the
remaining butter in a heavy-based pan.
Add the onion and pudding and cook
carefully. Season with salt and freshly
ground black pepper.

4. Once cooked, transfer the pudding and
onions to a clean serving dish and pour
the sauce over the top.

HOT SPICED BANANA WITH RUM AND SULTANA SAUCE

This is a recipe that can be made without too much effort and makes no apology for being very self-indulgent.

SERVES 4

4 large bananas
Juice of ½ lemon
4 tablespoons honey
4 tablespoons dark rum
Grated zest of 1 lemon
Grated zest of 1 orange
A pinch of cinnamon
A pinch of grated nutmeg
2 oz (50 g) sultanas
4 tablespoons grapenuts
4 tablespoons apricot jam
2 teaspoons arrowroot

1. Pre-heat the oven to gas mark 5, 375°F (190°C).

2. Peel the bananas and slice them in half across the centre to give 2 short, full-rounded pieces. Place them in a lightly buttered shallow ovenproof casserole.

3. Pour the lemon juice over them to prevent them from browning. Cover them with the honey and add the rum, grated lemon and orange zest, spices and sultanas.

4. Sprinkle with the grapenuts and cover with foil. Bake in the oven for 15 to 20 minutes until the grapenuts are crisp and brown.

5. Heat the apricot jam and carefully pour the cooking liquid into it. Bring this to the boil. Add a little cold water to the arrowroot and gradually whisk it into the liquid. Remove from the heat and pour over the bananas. Serve immediately.

═══ HOT SOUFFLÉ OF EXOTIC FRUITS ═══

I believe that for just a little effort, a soufflé gives a great amount of pleasure. In this recipe the fruits are enhanced as they have absorbed the flavour of the Cointreau before being baked in the soufflé. There are no hard and fast rules as to which fruits to use: select the best quality and value, but do be adventurous.

SERVES 6

1 small mango, peeled and diced
2 kiwi fruits, peeled and diced
3 slices pineapple, diced
3 passion fruit, flesh scooped out
4 tablespoons Cointreau
10 fl oz (300 ml) milk
4 oz (100 g) caster sugar
1 oz (25 g) plain flour
1½ oz (40 g) butter
Juice of ½ lemon
6 egg yolks
9 egg whites, whisked to a peak
Icing sugar to garnish

1. Place the prepared fruits in a bowl, add the Cointreau and place in the refrigerator for at least 1 hour.

2. Reserve 4 tablespoons of milk, place the rest in a pan and bring to the boil. Add the sugar, stir well, then remove from the heat.

3. Mix the reserved cold milk with the flour to a smooth paste. Gradually add this to the hot milk. Return to a low heat and stir for 4 minutes. Leave to cool for 5 minutes.

4. Add the butter, lemon juice and egg yolks and mix well. Transfer to a clean, large mixing bowl and leave to cool.

5. Pre-heat the oven to gas mark 7, 425°F (220°C).

6. Prepare 6 × 4-in (10-cm) soufflé moulds by lightly greasing them with softened butter. Sprinkle a little caster sugar over the inner surface and then divide the soaked fruit between them.

7. Using a metal spoon, fold the beaten egg whites into the soufflé mixture. Pour the mixture into the soufflé moulds.

8. Bake in the oven for 18 to 20 minutes until risen and golden brown. Sieve a little icing sugar over the surface and serve immediately.

CHERRY CLAFOUTIS

You can use different fruit, if you wish, for this dish. I usually serve it with a bowl of crème fraîche.

SERVES 4

1 lb (450 g) ripe cherries
8 oz (225 g) self-raising flour
3 eggs, lightly beaten
3 oz (75 g) caster sugar
4 fl oz (120 ml) milk
1 tablespoon kirsch

1. Pre-heat the oven to gas mark 4, 350°F (180°C).

2. Pick, wash and dry the cherries. Remove the stems and stones.

3. Sieve the flour into a bowl and make a well in the centre. Add the beaten eggs, 2 oz (50 g) of sugar, the milk and kirsch. Stir the liquid into the flour to form a smooth dough.

4. Strain the batter into a lightly buttered 10-in (25-cm) flan dish. Sprinkle the cherries into the batter and bake in the oven for 45 minutes to 1 hour until golden brown.

5. Sprinkle the remaining sugar over the surface and serve hot or cold.

RICH CHOCOLATE MOUSSE
ON WHITE CHOCOLATE SAUCE

Pure edible sin! Be sure to leave sufficient time afterwards to put your feet up, crash out by the fire and sleep this one off.

SERVES 4

8 oz (225 g) dark dessert chocolate
4 egg yolks
2 egg whites, beaten to soft peak stage
4 fl oz (120 ml) double cream, lightly whipped
1 large glass Cointreau
6 oz (175 g) white dessert chocolate
4 fl oz (120 ml) single cream
Grated zest of 1 orange
2 walnuts, halved

1. Melt the dark chocolate in a microwave or in a bowl over a pan of water. Once it has melted and is smooth, add the egg yolks.

2. Allow to cool slightly, then fold in the egg whites followed by the double cream and Cointreau.

3. Place the mixture in a refrigerator for at least 2 hours.

4. Prepare the sauce by melting the white chocolate. Allow it to cool, then add the single cream.

5. Pour the sauce on to a large serving plate.

6. Mould the dark chocolate mousse into quenelle shapes using two dessert spoons. Place them on to the white sauce and garnish with orange zest and walnuts.

CHOCOLATE AND COFFEE TORTE

This is my favourite afternoon pudding!

SERVES 6–8

3 oz (75 g) butter
3 oz (75 g) caster sugar
1 small glass sweet sherry
2 oz (50 g) cocoa powder
2 oz (50 g) walnut pieces
32 sponge fingers
5 fl oz (150 ml) hot black coffee
5 fl oz (150 ml) whipping cream
½ oz (15 g) coffee beans to decorate
½ oz (15 g) whole walnuts

1. Line an 8-in (20-cm) loose-bottomed flan ring or cake tin with kitchen foil.

2. Cream the butter and sugar together until light and fluffy then stir in the sherry, cocoa and walnut pieces. The mixture should be light enough to spread easily; if not, add a little more sherry.

3. Lay half the sponge fingers, sugar side up, in the flan ring and thoroughly dampen with half the coffee.

4. Cover the soaked biscuits completely with half the chocolate mix then arrange another layer of biscuits on top.

5. Carefully dampen each biscuit with the remaining coffee using a large spoon, then cover with the remainder of the filling.

6. Smooth the surface and chill, preferably overnight, until set.

7. Just before serving, whip the cream until thickened but still spreadable. Remove the torte from the tin and cover the top and sides with the cream.

8. Decorate with the coffee beans and whole walnuts.

TRIM CUISINE

If recipes ever needed to be inspirational, I believe it has to be in this chapter. It always seems to be the case that everything delicious, delightful and desirable, is also full of calories. Of course, all foods contain calories, but why is it that the foods we like best carry more than the others. Diet is by the nature of the topic, a very individual thing and it is virtually impossible to offer a package which will suit everyone, but the essential elements to note include a reduction in all fatty foods, oils, butters, margarines, sugar, sweets, chocolates, fried foods, cakes, biscuits, pastries, sweet drinks and, of course, alcohol.

It is unnecessary to exclude bread and potatoes from your diet; they serve a useful purpose by giving a feeling of fulfilment and therefore help to prevent a further intake of calories.

A sensible diet will also include plenty of fruit, vegetables, (raw and cooked), salads, wholemeal bread, pasta, brown rice, baked potatoes, cereals, lean meat, skinned white fish, poultry and low fat cheese. Effective weight loss and control requires will power, daily exercise, a sensible eating plan and the support of those around you.

CLEAR BEEF AND CELERY SOUP

In this soup the egg white (albumen) acts with the shin of beef to clarify the stock. Take great care not to disturb the 'nest' that forms on the surface of the soup or you will lose the clarity of the finished dish.

SERVES 4

8 oz (225 g) minced shin of
  beef
12 oz (350 g) celery, sliced
4 oz (100 g) carrots, peeled
  and sliced
4 oz (100 g) onions, peeled
  and sliced
4 oz (100 g) leeks, sliced
3 egg whites
1 tablespoon cold water
6 black peppercorns
1 bouquet garni
3 pints (1.75 litres) good
  brown stock
Salt
½ onion, peeled

1. Place the beef in a large pan. Slice 8 oz (225 g) of the celery and add it to the pan with the carrots, sliced onions and leeks and mix together.

2. Add the egg whites and cold water and ensure that they are well mixed through the meat.

3. Add the peppercorns, bouquet garni and stock, season lightly with salt and gradually bring the liquid to the boil.

4. Meanwhile place the peeled ½ onion into a deep frying pan and allow the cut surface to burn. Once black, add this to the soup without disturbing the packed meat and vegetables (this will enhance the colour of the consommé).

5. Allow the soup to simmer for 45 minutes. Meanwhile, chop and cook the remaining celery.

6. When the soup is cooked, ladle the liquid very carefully through a conical strainer covered with a muslin cloth.

7. Check and adjust the seasoning if necessary, then serve garnished with the cooked celery.

TIMBALE OF COURGETTE WITH SPINACH AND BACON FILLING

This dish can serve as a starter for the whole family and they wouldn't feel as though they were participants in your controlled diet as the dish appears so substantial.

SERVES 4

3 courgettes
3 large carrots, peeled
2½ lb (1.25 kg) spinach,
  washed, trimmed and
  chopped
Salt and freshly ground
  black pepper
A pinch of grated nutmeg
3 fl oz (75 ml) plain
  yoghurt
1 egg yolk, lightly beaten
2 oz (50 g) bacon, rind
  removed, finely diced and
  cooked
1 small lettuce, washed and
  chopped
4 fl oz (120 ml) chicken
  stock
4 oz (100 g) shredded
  carrot, cooked

1. Top and tail the courgettes and, using a potato peeler, peel them lengthways into thin slices. Do the same with the carrots. Place them into separate pans of boiling salted water and blanch until soft.

2. Pre-heat the oven to gas mark 5, 375°F (190°C).

3. Lightly butter 4 individual dariole moulds and line them with the blanched carrot and courgette, alternating and slightly overlapping the vegetables.

4. Blanch and drain the spinach. Season with salt, freshly ground black pepper and nutmeg.

5. Mix in the yoghurt, egg yolk and bacon.

6. Pack the spinach mixture into the lined darioles and cover the top with carrot and courgette. Seal with kitchen foil.

7. Place into a roasting tray, half filled with water, and cook in the oven for 20 to 30 minutes.

8. Add the chopped lettuce to the chicken stock and cook for 4 minutes over a medium heat. Purée the lettuce and stock in a food processor, season with salt and freshly ground black pepper and keep warm until required.

9. When ready to serve, strain the lettuce sauce on to 4 plates.

10. Carefully remove the timbales from the darioles (allow them to drain for a moment or two on a clean cloth before putting them on to the plate).

11. Place them on the sauce, garnish with the shredded carrot and serve.

SALAD CAPRICE

A combination of crisp chilled lettuce with market-fresh prawns and slightly over-ripe melon bound together with a tomato yoghurt – gastronomic poetry!

SERVES 4

½ small lettuce
8 oz (225 g) prawns, cooked and peeled
1 small ripe melon, deseeded
Salt and freshly ground black pepper
5 fl oz (150 ml) plain yoghurt
Grated zest and juice of ½ lemon
1 tablespoon tomato purée
½ teaspoon Worcestershire sauce
2 drops tabasco sauce
4 tomatoes, skinned, deseeded and finely chopped
2 lemons, quartered
2 tablespoons snipped chives

1. Wash and finely shred the lettuce.

2. Place the prawns in a bowl. Scoop out the melon flesh using a parisienne cutter and add to the prawns. Season lightly with salt and freshly ground black pepper.

3. Mix together the yoghurt, lemon zest and juice and tomato purée. Season with salt, freshly ground black pepper, Worcestershire and tabasco sauce. Pour this over the prawns and melon and mix together.

4. Arrange the shredded lettuce in the centre of a large plate, place some of the prawn and melon mixture on the lettuce and garnish with a spoonful of the chopped tomato, quarters of lemon and top the mixture with some snipped chives.

CHICKEN BREASTS WITH CASSEROLE OF DEVILLED PIMENTO

This is a dish where it is advisable to know the likes or dislikes of your guest very well. Then you will know just how hot to make the devilled pimento!

SERVES 4

3 oz (75 g) celery, sliced
3 oz (75 g) carrots, peeled
  and sliced
2 oz (50 g) leek, sliced
5 oz (150 g) onions, peeled
  and sliced
4 black peppercorns
1 bouquet garni
15 fl oz (450 ml) chicken
  stock
Salt
4 chicken breasts, skin and
  fat removed
1 tablespoon vegetable oil
1 clove garlic, peeled and
  crushed
4 oz (100 g) button
  mushrooms, finely diced
1 teaspoon freshly crushed
  black peppercorns
1½ large green peppers
  (pimentos), chopped
1½ large red peppers
  (pimentos), chopped
2 tomatoes, skinned,
  deseeded and diced
1 tablespoon chopped basil
1 small glass dry white
  wine
2 drops tabasco sauce

1. Place the celery, carrots, leek, 2 oz (50 g) of onion, the peppercorns and bouquet garni in the stock and simmer for 5 minutes. Season very lightly with salt.

2. Immerse the chicken breasts in the stock and simmer gently until cooked.

3. Meanwhile, heat the oil in a separate pan. Chop the remaining onion and fry it with the garlic, for 2 minutes, without colouring. Add the mushrooms, crushed peppercorns, green and red peppers, diced tomatoes and basil. Cook for a further 4 minutes, stirring gently and frequently.

4. Add the wine and simmer to reduce by two-thirds.

5. Season to taste with the tabasco sauce, Worcestershire sauce, salt and if necessary more freshly ground black pepper.

6. Transfer the pepper dish into 4 lightly greased ramekins and cover.

7. Remove the chicken, cover and keep hot. Increase the heat under the stock and allow to reduce by half.

8. For the sorrel cream, sauté the mushrooms and sorrel in the stock for 5 minutes, then stir in the yoghurt or quark and heat through without boiling.

3 drops Worcestershire
sauce

For the sorrel cream:
4 oz (100 g) mushrooms,
sliced
2 oz (50 g) sorrel leaves,
finely chopped
5 fl oz (150 ml) chicken
stock
3 tablespoons plain
yoghurt or quark

9. Unmould the casseroles of peppers on to the centre of a large serving plate, cut the supremes of chicken into collops across the breast and arrange overlapping around the pimento. Moisten the chicken with the reduced stock, garnish with the cooked vegetables and serve with the mushrooms and sorrel.

RAINBOW TROUT IN WINE AND CUCUMBER STOCK

This simple presentation allows the natural flavour and beauty of this fish to shine through.

SERVES 4

4 medium-sized trout
6 fl oz (175 ml) dry white
wine
Salt and freshly ground
black pepper
½ bay leaf
Grated zest and juice of ½
lemon
½ cucumber, peeled and
diced
1 oz (25 g) butter, chilled
1 sprig of parsley
½ lemon, sliced

1. Pre-heat the oven to gas mark 6, 400°F (200°C).

2. Wash and clean the trout, remove the eyes and fins and place in a shallow casserole. Add the wine and season lightly with salt and freshly ground black pepper. Add the bay leaf and lemon juice. Cover and cook in the oven for about 15 minutes until cooked.

3. Remove the trout from the dish and keep it warm. Remove and discard the bay leaf.

4. Bring the stock to the boil, add the cucumber and lemon zest. Remove from the heat and slowly stir in the cold butter.

5. Pour the sauce over the trout and garnish with the sliced lemon and parsley.

DICED TOFU WITH CHINESE-STYLE SPICED VEGETABLES

This low-calorie dish has the advantage of a high protein count gained from the tofu, a soya bean product which is available from most good health food shops.

SERVES 4

1 tablespoon corn oil
1 onion, peeled and sliced
4 oz (100 g) carrots, peeled
  and thinly sliced
1 green pepper, deseeded
  and diced
1 red pepper, deseeded and
  diced
1 head Chinese leaves,
  coarsely chopped
4 spring onions, washed
  and diced
2 oz (50 g) mushrooms,
  sliced
8 oz (225 g) tofu, diced
2 tablespoons soy sauce
Salt and freshly ground
  black pepper
A pinch of allspice

1. Heat the oil in a wide, shallow pan. Add the onion, and cook for 1 minute. Add the carrots and cook for a further 3 minutes.

2. Add the green and red peppers, Chinese leaves, spring onions and mushrooms. Cook, stirring frequently, for 4 minutes.

3. Add the tofu and then the soy sauce. Season lightly with salt, freshly ground black pepper and a pinch of allspice and cook for 2 minutes, stirring frequently. Serve immediately.

POACHED FILLET OF BEEF AND SALSIFY WITH MADEIRA REDUCTION

A small portion of beef fillet lightly poached in a good stock with additional vegetables makes for a lovely main course. The addition of salsify to the recipe adds a new dimension to the dish.

SERVES 4

1 lb (450 g) salsify
Juice of 1 lemon
1 tablespoon plain flour
Salt and freshly ground
  black pepper
1 lb (450 g) trimmed beef
  fillet
1¼ pints (750 ml) brown
  beef stock
4 oz (100 g) onions, peeled
  and sliced
4 oz (100 g) carrots, peeled
  and sliced
4 oz (100 g) celery, sliced
4 oz (100 g) leeks, sliced
1 bouquet garni
1 tablespoon cornflour
1 small glass madeira

1. Wash and peel the salsify and cut into 2-in (5-cm) long pieces. Cook in a pan of boiling water containing the lemon juice, plain flour and a little salt for about 40 to 45 minutes until cooked.

2. Meanwhile, season the fillet lightly with salt and freshly ground black pepper and place to one side. Pre-heat the oven to gas mark 6, 400°F (200°C).

3. Place the stock in a flameproof casserole dish just large enough to hold the fillet. Add the vegetables and bring to the boil. Lay the fillet in the stock, add the bouquet garni, cover and cook in the oven for about 15 to 20 minutes. (The time is dependent upon how you like your meat cooked.)

4. Drain the salsify and keep it hot.

5. Remove the meat from the liquid and keep it warm. Dilute the cornflour with a little water. Bring the liquid to the boil and whisk in the cornflour. Remove the bouquet garni and add the madeira.

6. Lay the fillet on a warm, deep serving dish, pour over the sauce and vegetables and place 4 bouquets of salsify on the dish.

FRUIT-FILLED BAKED APPLES WITH NUTMEG YOGHURT

Select large firm cooking apples and feel free to use whatever dried fruit takes your fancy.

SERVES 4

4 cooking apples
3 oz (75 g) dried dates, chopped
3 oz (75 g) dried apricots, chopped
Grated zest of 1 lemon
Grated zest and juice of ½ orange
2 tablespoons honey
10 fl oz (300 ml) plain yoghurt
Pinch of grated nutmeg

1. Pre-heat the oven to gas mark 4, 350°F (180°C).

2. Neatly slice off the top of the apples and retain.

3. Remove the cores and, using a teaspoon, take out some of the apple to a depth of about 1 in (2.5 cm). Make an incision around the middle of the apples, piercing the skin, and sit the apples in an ovenproof dish containing 4 tablespoons of cold water.

4. Place the dried fruit in a bowl, add the lemon zest, orange juice and honey. Mix well and place the mixture into the apples. Replace the tops.

5. Bake in the oven for 35 to 45 minutes until the apples are cooked through.

6. Mix together the yoghurt, orange zest and nutmeg and serve with the apples.

CRÈME BRULÉE WITH CHILLED EXOTIC FRUIT

This is a super alternative to the classic recipe.

SERVES 4

4 oz (100 g) pineapple, finely diced

3 oz (75 g) mango, peeled and finely diced

3 oz (75 g) kiwi fruit, peeled, quartered and sliced

1 tablespoon kirsch

5 fl oz (150 ml) whipping cream

5 fl oz (150 ml) Greek yoghurt, strained

1 oz (25 g) golden granulated sugar

1. Mix the prepared fruit with the kirsch and divide equally between 4 small ramekins.

2. Whip the cream until it forms soft peaks and fold in the yoghurt. Spoon the mixture over the fruit and ensure that the surface is smooth. Cover and chill in the refrigerator for 2 hours.

3. Sprinkle the sugar over the surface of each dish and place under the grill until the sugar browns.

CARROT AND BANANA CAKE

This sugar-free cake is sweetened by the grated carrot.

SERVES 8 (OR 4 GREEDY
DIETERS!)

**6 oz (175 g) carrots, peeled
and grated**
**6 oz (175 g) self-raising
wholemeal flour**
**2 small bananas, peeled and
mashed**
**2 fl oz (50 ml) fresh orange
juice**
Grated zest of 1 orange
3 oz (75 g) sultanas
1 teaspoon baking powder
½ teaspoon mixed spice
2 oz (50 g) flaked almonds

1. Pre-heat the oven to gas mark 4, 350°F
(180°C).

2. Place all the ingredients in a bowl and
beat until thoroughly mixed.

3. Transfer into a greased and lined 8-in
(20-cm) cake tin.

4. Bake in the oven for about 1 hour. Test
to see if it is cooked by inserting a skewer
or needle into the centre of the cake.
Once removed, it should be clean and free
from batter.

5. Once cooked, remove from the tin and
leave to cool on a wire rack.

HEART ATTACK CUISINE

Most of us today show an interest in the effect that diet plays upon the body and there has been, over the last few years, particular attention drawn to food and its effect on the heart. The British Heart Foundation suggest that meat with a high proportion of polyunsaturated fat, such as lean pork and ham, do less damage than lamb and beef, so when choosing the latter, select very lean cuts and remove any surplus hard fats before cooking.

There is much sense in bulking out the meat portion using beans, pasta and vegetables and avoiding high fat products such as sausages and pork pies. Egg yolk is very high in cholesterol so eggs should be limited to no more than 3 a week. Use low fat dairy products such as low fat cheese, low fat spreads instead of butter, skimmed milk in preference to full cream, and try and avoid, like the plague, rich creamy sauces and baked goods such as conventional cakes and biscuits. In essence a diet for a healthy heart should be high in vegetables, rice, pasta, wholegrain cereals and bread with evidence of less saturated fat, low in full fat dairy products, red meat and meat products. The cooking style should exclude frying and you should always remove as much fat from ingredients before and after cooking as possible. But do remember – eating is an essential element in life's playground, and consideration given to a healthy diet mustn't mean boring meal times. So, be bold with your cooking and selective with your ingredients.

Chilled Cucumber Soup

This is the simplest soup recipe imaginable, yet the finished result is so clean and refreshing.

SERVES 4

½ large cucumber
4 fl oz (120 ml) plain
 yoghurt
2 fl oz (50 ml) milk
2 fl oz (50 ml) soured cream
1 teaspoon chopped
 tarragon
Juice of ¼ lemon
Salt and freshly ground
 black pepper

1. Peel the cucumber, discarding the skin, and cut 8 thin slices.

2. Place the rest of the cucumber into a food processor, add the yoghurt, milk and soured cream, and season with tarragon, lemon juice, salt and freshly ground black pepper.

3. Blend until smooth.

4. Chill in the refrigerator.

5. Garnish with cucumber slices just before serving.

Scotch Broth

A real Highland soup – full of goodness – this adaptation uses a lean cut of lamb and not so much of it, so it's a 'wee' bit more expensive, but much better for you.

SERVES 4–6

1 tablespoon olive oil
2 lamb cutlets, all fat and gristle removed
1½ oz (40 g) pearl barley, rinsed
3 oz (75 g) carrots, peeled and diced
3 oz (75 g) turnip, peeled and diced
3 oz (75 g) onions, peeled and diced
4 oz (100 g) leeks, diced
4 oz (100 g) white cabbage, thinly sliced
1 tablespoon chopped parsley
2½ pints (1.5 litres) chicken stock
Salt and freshly ground black pepper
1 bouquet garni

1. Heat the oil in a very large, heavy-based pan. Add the cutlets and seal on both sides. Remove them from the pan and put to one side.

2. Add the pearl barley and vegetables to the hot pan and cook for 5 minutes, stirring frequently.

3. Add the meat, parsley, chicken stock and bouquet garni. Bring to the boil, cover with a tight-fitting lid and simmer for 40 to 50 minutes.

4. Once the meat and vegetables are cooked, remove the cutlets from the soup. Cut the meat into small pieces and return to the soup.

5. Remove and discard the bouquet garni. Check and adjust the seasoning if necessary and serve.

═ Smoked Mackerel and Gherkin Pâté ═

I actually prefer the flavour and coarseness of smoked mackerel to smoked salmon – I certainly prefer the price! This recipe avoids the use of cream which is found in most fish pâtés buy using bread and skimmed milk.

SERVES 4

1 lb (450 g) smoked mackerel
3 oz (75 g) soft white breadcrumbs
6 tablespoons skimmed milk
Grated zest of 1 lemon
Juice of ½ lemon
1 tablespoons chopped parsley
A pinch of paprika
Freshly ground black pepper
4 oz (100 g) gherkins, finely diced

1. Ensure that the mackerel is free from skin and bones and break the flesh into small pieces.

2. Place the fish, breadcrumbs, milk, lemon zest and juice into a food processor or blender and process to a smooth pâté.

3. Season with parsley, paprika and freshly ground black pepper. Remove from the machine.

4. Add the diced gherkins and mix in well. Divide the pâté into small ramekins and chill in the refrigerator.

5. Serve well chilled with brown bread and butter.

Seafood Indiènne

This is an ideal dish to make when the fish you have is not particularly attractive. You can use any oily fish or even several different types that take your fancy.

SERVES 4

1 tablespoon olive oil
3 oz (75 g) onions, peeled
  and finely chopped
1 clove garlic, peeled and
  crushed
3 oz (75 g) carrots, peeled
  and finely diced
2 oz (50 g) celery, finely
  diced
1 tablespoon curry powder
½ tablespoon plain flour
15 fl oz (450 ml) fish stock
1 oz (25 g) sultanas
3 oz (75 g) apple, peeled,
  cored and diced
1 lb (450 g) haddock or
  alternative fish, skinned
  and cut into 1-in (2.5-cm)
  dice
Juice of ½ lemon
Salt and freshly ground
  black pepper

1. Heat the oil, add the onions and garlic and cook gently for 3 minutes. Add the carrots and celery and cook for 2 minutes. Sprinkle the curry powder over the surface and mix well.

2. Add the flour to absorb any surplus fat, mix in well, then gradually mix in the stock. Bring this to the boil, turn down the heat and add the sultanas, apple, fish and lemon juice. Cook very gently for 15 to 20 minutes.

3. Season to taste with salt and freshly ground black pepper and serve with brown rice and a selection of crudités.

STEAMED FILLET OF TURBOT ON SPINACH MOUSSE WITH TENDER VEGETABLES

This style of cookery was traditionally only for invalids. In my opinion, it is one of the nicest ways to cook a piece of fresh fish. It's gentle, whilst allowing the fish to retain moisture and flavour during cooking.

SERVES 4

1½ lb (750 g) fresh spinach, washed
A pinch of grated nutmeg
Salt and freshly ground black pepper
1½ lb (750 g) fresh mixed baby vegetables
4 × 4-oz (100-g) fillets of turbot
2 lemons, halved

1. Pick out enough leaves of spinach to line 4 small ramekins, blanch and dry them.

2. Very lightly grease 4 ramekins and cover the inside with the spinach leaves. Chop the remaining leaves and cook in a minimum amount of water. Drain well and season with nutmeg, salt and freshly ground black pepper. Pack into the ramekins, cover and keep warm.

3. Cook the baby vegetables until tender, then drain.

4. Place the fish in a Chinese wicker basket over a pan of water, or on a plate covered with a top plate set over a pan of water. Season lightly with salt and freshly ground black pepper and steam for 5 to 8 minutes until cooked.

5. Turn out the spinach mousse, place the fish gently over the mousse and surround with the vegetables.

6. Garnish with lemon.

Cod Braised with Leeks in Cider

A lovely combination of flavours is gained from the cider and leeks which perfectly complements the fish.

SERVES 4

1 tablespoon sunflower oil
2 oz (50 g) onion, peeled
 and finely chopped
4 oz (100 g) leeks, diced
1 lb (450 g) cod, skinned
 and cut into 2-in (5-cm)
 pieces
Salt and freshly ground
 black pepper
10 fl oz (300 ml) cider
Juice of ½ lemon
4 fl oz (120 ml) milk
½ oz (15 g) butter

1. Heat the oil in a large frying pan. Add the onion and leek and cook for 3 to 4 minutes. Add the fish pieces, season to taste with salt and freshly ground black pepper and cover with the cider. Bring to the boil, reduce the heat, cover and simmer for 6 to 8 minutes until the fish is cooked through.

2. Remove the fish and vegetables from the liquid with a slotted spoon, cover with kitchen foil and keep warm. Bring the cooking liquid to the boil, add the lemon juice and milk and continue boiling until one-third of the liquid has evaporated. Remove from the heat and whisk in the butter.

3. Check and adjust the seasoning if necessary.

4. Pour the sauce over the fish and vegetables and serve at once.

Poached Halibut with White Wine and Mushroom Sauce

Halibut could be classed as the ocean's answer to a good rump steak. It has all the qualities of a very substantial piece of meat without the associated health problems.

SERVES 4

4 × 6-oz (175-g) halibut steaks
4 oz (100 g) onions, peeled and finely chopped
1½ tablespoons chopped parsley
6 oz (175 g) button mushrooms, sliced
Salt and freshly ground black pepper
4 tablespoons dry white wine
10 fl oz (300 ml) plain yoghurt

1. Pre-heat the oven to gas mark 4, 350°F (180°C).

2. Place the halibut steaks in an ovenproof dish and sprinkle on the onion, 1 tablespoon of parsley and the mushrooms.

3. Season lightly with salt and freshly ground black pepper. Pour on the wine and cover with a lid.

4. Bake in the oven for 40 to 45 minutes until the fish is cooked.

5. Drain the cooking liquid into a clean saucepan, add the yoghurt and bring slowly to the boil.

6. Check and adjust the seasoning if necessary. Pour the sauce over the fish and garnish with just a little chopped parsley.

HERRINGS IN TOMATO AND GARLIC SAUCE

Select herrings which look moist (covered in a sea slime) with flat scales, a fresh smell and bulging eyes. It is also useful to use a fishmonger who is prepared to spend time to fillet the fish for you.

SERVES 4

4 herrings, cleaned and filleted
Salt and freshly ground black pepper
Juice of 1 lemon
A few parsley stalks
1 tablespoon olive oil
2 cloves garlic, peeled and crushed
3 oz (75 g) onions, peeled and finely chopped
1 × 14-oz (400-g) tin chopped tomatoes
½ tablespoon chopped basil
1 tablespoon tomato purée
Salt and freshly ground black pepper
2 drops tabasco sauce
A pinch of sugar
1 tablespoon chopped parsley

1. Pre-heat the oven to gas mark 4, 350°F (180°C).

2. Wash and dry the fish fillets and place them in an ovenproof dish. Season them lightly with salt and freshly ground black pepper. Pour the lemon juice over the fish and add the parsley stalks. Cover and bake in the oven for 20 to 25 minutes until the herrings are cooked.

3. Heat the oil in a saucepan, add the garlic and onions. Cook for 3 minutes, then add the chopped tomatoes, basil and tomato purée. Cook for 4 minutes.

4. Season with salt, freshly ground black pepper, tabasco sauce (not too much) and sugar.

5. Remove the fish from the oven and carefully pour the cooking liquid into the tomato sauce.

6. Mix the sauce ingredients well and pour this over the fish. Garnish with a little freshly chopped parsley.

═══ Smoked Wild Duck Salad ═══ with Garlic and Rosemary Dressing

Duck, I hear you say! How could this recipe be included in this section. I'll tell you. Wild duck is very lean and as it is quite rich you can get away with small portions. The garlic has excellent properties for keeping the body healthy. Serve with a selection of fresh washed salad leaves of your choice such as oak leaf, frisée, radicchio, watercress or basil.

SERVES 4

Variety of salad leaves such as lamb's lettuce, oak leaf, radicchio, lollo rosso
1 lb (450 g) smoked wild duck breast, thinly sliced
3 fl oz (85 ml) walnut oil
1 fl oz (25 ml) wine vinegar
1 teaspoon French mustard
2 cloves garlic, peeled and crushed
1 tablespoon chopped rosemary
Freshly ground black pepper

1. Arrange a variety of leaves on a large serving plate.

2. Arrange the sliced duck breast around the outside of the leaves.

3. Blend the remaining ingredients and dress the salad just before serving.

Apricot and Sultana Brose

This is a pleasant adaptation of a good traditional Scottish sweet which normally uses double cream and whisky. It's possible to enjoy life without it – and life might even be longer!

SERVES 4

4 oz (100 g) dried apricots, diced
2 oz (50 g) sultanas
5 fl oz (300 ml) plain low fat yoghurt
1 tablespoon honey
Grated zest of 1 orange
6 tablespoons rolled oats, toasted

1. Mix all the ingredients except the oats in a bowl and place in a refrigerator to chill for at least 8 hours.

2. Divide the sweet into individual sweet dishes and top with the toasted rolled oats when ready to serve.

Index